SURRENDER

FROM DESPAIR TO DISCIPLE

Amy Sutton

NEW HARBOR PRESS

RAPID CITY, SD

Sutton/New HarborPress
1601 Mt. Rushmore Rd, Ste 3288
Rapid City, SD 57701
www.newharborpress.com

Ordering Information:
Quantity sales. Special discounts are available on quantity purchases by corporations, associations, and others. For details, contact the "Special Sales Department" at the address above.

Surrender/Amy Sutton. -- 1st ed.
ISBN 978-1-63357-440-3

Dedicated to
The Love of My Life – My God and My Savior
and
My beloved children –
Mikayla, Makenzi, Aiden, Damien, Dominik, Traeh, and Jeremiah
The LORD is your keeper,
and He will never leave you nor forsake you.
He loves you with a deep and everlasting love,
so trust in Him with all of your heart
and keep your eyes fixed upon Him!
I am praying for you always!
I Love You

.

Contents

INTRODUCTION

BEFORE WE BEGIN, I would like to take a moment to give credit where credit is due. To God be all the glory!

This book certainly did not come to fruition in my own strength nor has it come to fruition by my own will. I did not write this book simply because I wanted to write it but because I felt God compelling me to write it. He saw fit to reveal Himself to me, an unworthy servant, and it has now become my duty (and privilege) to record what great things He has done, though they are far more than can be told.

He brought every thought and every scripture to mind. Often, this would happen during my quiet moments spent with Him. At other times, this seemed to occur more randomly. It was in these moments I found myself frantically searching for a pen and a piece of paper, napkin, etc. How these various notes on several pieces of paper came together so fluidly, in and of itself, is nothing short of a miracle, and God gets every ounce of glory. I could not have done this without Him. Furthermore, I would not have done this if He had not nudged me and provided the material.

God has a plan for this book, and you were always a part of that plan. It is not by chance that you hold these pages in your hands. He had you in mind as He worked in me and through my fingertips. I pray that you will be encouraged to immerse yourself in the scriptures, that your relationship with Him will be strengthened, that you will be challenged to lay down idolatries in love and faithfulness to Him, and that you will be emboldened to disciple those special people He brings into your path. This book challenges the wisdom of this world by highlighting the wisdom of God's Word, and I pray that you are inspired to . . . *Surrender*.

CHAPTER ONE

Obedience Matters

Go, therefore, and make disciples of all nations . . .
teaching them to observe all that I have commanded You.
And behold, I am with you always
to the end of the age.
Matthew 28:19-20

SURRENDER IS A WORD that packs a mighty punch. By definition, it is to give up oneself into the power of another; to yield. In the
life of a Christian, it is a word which describes the beginning of true
transformation. We cannot grow and we will not begin our transformation apart from complete surrender. Surrendering my life and my
will with my whole heart, mind, and soul is where I began a journey
of testing and trusting, full of failures and victories, and a building of
courage and faith proven through action in the face of fear, adversity,
and opposition.

Even now, as I sit here and attempt to write this book, I am
praying for surrender of my thoughts and ideas and asking God to
put His words on paper. Done in my own so-called strength, these
writings will be ineffective and worthless. However, done in the awesome power of the Most High God, the possibilities of effect are limitless. As the enemy and my pride seek to overwhelm me or make me

quit this project in the face of obvious inadequacies, the conversation between the LORD and Moses echoes in my ear, and I know He says, "But I will be with you." Praise the LORD! For that which He has called us to do, He will enable us to accomplish, and He will supply every need according to His riches in glory.

Those of us who have chosen to follow Jesus Christ (Yeshua Hamashiach) serve a God without limitation. I think it is safe to say we all have a head knowledge of this truth. However, actions speak louder than words, and it is our actions which seem to be telling a different story as fear and worry often take precedence.

Our God is, of course, limitless, and He can do anything at any time in any way He chooses. Once we come to realize how deep His love runs for each one of us, we find He can be trusted completely. His sovereignty then becomes our greatest comfort. Nothing will happen to you or to me that God has not allowed, and if He has allowed it, He has a good reason for it. It is impossible for us to see or comprehend all that He sees and knows. However, we can trust that He loves us with an everlasting love, and we know that all things work together for good to them that love God and are called according to his purpose (Romans 8:28, KJV).

It is one thing to say things like nothing is impossible with God; He is for us, not against us; if God is for us, who can be against us; and nothing in all creation can separate us from the love of God. It is another thing entirely to live as though these words are absolute truth. Once we wholeheartedly embrace surrender and the truth of God's Word, total transformation can begin.

Unfortunately, there seems to be a considerable number of God's children living as if the Word of God is not all that important;

it is more of an afterthought or maybe not a thought at all. This was true for me. I did not understand His ability or His desire to powerfully speak through His Word in a personal way. God's Word is so extraordinary that it transcends economic/social status, varying levels of trauma, different stages of maturity, gender, culture, whatever. It does not matter! God uses the exact same Word to speak to each of us in a way that is specific and direct to our individual circumstances and need. It is powerful. It is beautiful. It is the very Word of God. So shall my Word be that goes out from my mouth; it shall not return to me empty, but it shall accomplish that which I purpose and shall succeed in the thing for which I sent it (Isaiah 55:11).

We are not without responsibility as we read the Word of God. In order to unlock the power of the scriptures, we must aim for obedience to it. We are called to be doers of the Word and not hearers only (James 1:22). Obedience is not the reason we are accepted and loved by God, and I want to make that clear. Obedience should be, however, our response to our relationship with Him because we realize we are already fully loved, forgiven, and accepted through the precious blood of Christ. I love my God, and I desire to be loyal to Him. I do not desire to take part in the things which are detestable in His sight, so I strive for obedience to His commands.

So, how do we know for certain what these commands are and what they are not? By hanging on His every Word. Why? Because there are many opinions floating around that do not have a biblical foundation. And why should we obey? Because of love – His love for me and my love for Him.

The Word of God is living and active, sharper than any two-edged sword . . . discerning the thoughts and intentions of the heart

(Hebrews 4:12). As God convicts us through His Word, we ought to pray that He would give us the ability to obey what we have read. Apart from Him, we can do nothing, and it is God who gives us the ability to obey. We must seek His help and His strength to be successful. The spirit, indeed, is willing, but the flesh is so weak. Fortunately, if we ask anything within the will of God, we know we have that for which we have asked. You can be sure that our obedience is within His perfect will.

It is within this realm of obedience that we are able to move from spiritual infancy to spiritual maturity, out of the shallow and into the deep. As Paul writes, we are being transformed into the same image from *one degree of glory to another.* The more obedient we become to His Word, the more truth He will reveal to us. When that revelation leads to further obedience, that obedience will lead to further revelation, and so on. If this cycle is disrupted, and repentance and restoration does not take place, our spiritual growth will be stunted and may even begin to decline. As God reveals our disobedience to us, we must repent and return. If we stubbornly continue in our disobedience, we are sure to reap disaster. Blessed is the one who fears the LORD always, but whoever hardens his heart will fall into calamity (Proverbs 28:14).

The LORD disciplines those He loves, and He will not allow you to continue along this path of destruction. Today, if you hear His voice, do not harden your hearts as in the rebellion on the day of testing in the wilderness. These things took place as examples for us that we might not desire evil as they did (I Corinthians 10:6).

Refusing to be obedient to the Word of God leads to a hardness of heart and a going astray. Our lives begin to look no different from the lives of the many lost souls around us, and the sin of disobedience (rebellion) begins to drive a wedge. Consequently, our relationship/intimacy with God suffers. Behold, to obey is better than sacrifice and to listen than the fat of rams for rebellion is as the sin of divination (I Samuel 15:23). He remains faithful, but we will slip further into our unfaithfulness. Rebellion is a disgusting slap in the face to our Savior and will lead to a life absent of any lasting fruitfulness, not to mention devoid of peace and joy.

In order to discover what true obedience looks like, we must know the Word of God. With my whole heart, I seek you. Let me not wander from your commandments. I have stored up your Word in my heart that I might not sin against you (Psalm 119:10-11). It is imperative that we seek God through His Word for ourselves and allow the Spirit of God to interpret the content to us personally. All your children shall be taught by the LORD and great shall be the peace of your children (Isaiah 54:13). We have the incredible gift of the Holy Spirit, who leads us into all truth and brings truth to remembrance at just the right moment. As He does this, we must be careful not to quench the Holy Spirit, thereby grieving the Holy Spirit. The more we quench the voice of God, the less we hear the voice of God until we hear His voice no more.

Some of you may be proclaiming Christianity yet failing to follow Christ. There are far too many believers living life on their own terms, living in disobedience, and enslaved and in bondage to sin. Refusing to obey the truth, they have become dull of hearing and completely indifferent to the Word of God. If this is striking a chord somewhere within, there is hope. This was my story up until roughly three years ago. Therefore, lift your drooping hands and strengthen your weak knees and make straight paths for your feet, so that what is lame may not be put out of joint, but rather be healed (Hebrews 12:12-13).

Lacking in true humility and total surrender to my Lord Jesus Christ, I spent more than thirty years as an infant Christian, always learning yet never able to arrive at a knowledge of the truth. In fact, there were some years my life looked anything but Christian. You might not have thought I was a child of God by the way I was acting. You may be thinking, well, maybe you were not a child of God at all. After laying this inquiry before the LORD, I am confident today that I was, in fact, given the gift of the Holy Spirit as a guarantee many years ago. I had wisdom and discernment from a young age which could have only come from above, and it was obvious that His Law was written on my heart and mind. Looking back, I am certain I had a strong connection to Him early on. This reality makes my apostasy even more revolting. It is not, however, unlike the stories we read in the scriptures regarding the apostasy of the ancient Israelites. In his faithful lovingkindness, He never gave up on me. Praise the LORD! Though I felt God's calling many times to repent and return to Him, to turn from my evil ways and amend my ways and my deeds, I said in my heart, that is in vain! I will follow my own plans and act according to the stubbornness of my evil heart (Jeremiah 18:11-12).

Growing up, my parents took me to church, and I heard about the truth and the love of God; however, what I experienced at home was not a loving, Christian environment. It was, as most homes are, dysfunctional. My dad was an alcoholic and a workaholic, and my mom was bent on trying to micromanage and control everyone and everything. Repeatedly, I had to plead with my dad not to kill himself, and this was but one of the many miserable burdens I was forced to carry from a very young age.

When I was 7 years old, I repented the best I knew how and made a public declaration that I wanted to follow Jesus Christ. The same spirit who raised Jesus from the dead, the Spirit of God, came to live inside of me. The symbolic picture of baptism was explained to me, and I was baptized. This eager desire to commit to the LORD was not nurtured through discipleship, and home life was still fraught with dysfunction and misery. Being raised in this hypocrisy coupled with that seed of rebellion was a recipe for disaster. Like the seed that fell on the rocky ground and immediately sprung up, so was the Word of God in my life, but when the sun arose, it was scorched, and since there was no root to withstand trial and tribulation, it withered away (see Matthew 13:5-6).

By the age of 13, I had endured more than I could handle. I was now filled with self-destructive rage and living on the street as a prostitute seemed more attractive than living another day with my parents. I stole their car and ran away in the middle of the night. Sixteen or so hours later, I was pulled over and apprehended. I was expelled from eighth grade and admitted to a psychiatric hospital for a few weeks. Afterward, my mom took me to see a counselor. I cannot recall the conversation in that first session, but it was my last. After speaking with me, she spoke with my mom privately. Later in life, my mom told me that she went in there desperate for someone to "fix" me, but to her shock, the counselor said, "I don't need to see your daughter; I need to see you." This was a turning point for my mom, which would start her on her own journey to seek God with all of her heart. Praise the LORD! Of course, transformation does not happen overnight for any of us, and I was, by this point, mad at the world, wishing for death, and completely and hopelessly depressed.

Not knowing what to do with me, my parents sent me to another state where I stayed with some friends of our family while attending ninth grade. I continued in my rebellion and, indeed, found new ways to sin. When I moved back home, this rebellion, which included drug and alcohol use, quickly escalated. Subsequently, I was sent to a group home for one year, which included another short stint in a psychiatric ward in the midst of that year.

I got out of the group home at age 16 and continued to seek out ways of escape. This time I would discover the needle, and no, I do not mean crochet. Of course, that lifestyle does not come without danger and abuse. How many times I would plead with God, "Just don't let me wake up." Staying up for weeks at a time and sleeping for two or three days at a time became the cycle. I was surrounded by demonic activity that I could feel and hear. I was grieving the Holy Spirit in every possible way, and I was extremely miserable. I was beaten and broken, accused, and spit on. I stared down the barrel of a gun more than once, and I was no stranger to having a knife to my throat or chest. I was even drenched in kerosene from head to toe and threatened with a match. The physical and mental abuse was frequent and demonic. I could have gone home, but the so-called "freedom" and "escape" it provided kept me out there. Of course, it was not freedom at all. It was not even truly escape. It was a deep, dark bondage to sin and idolatry. Oh, how my apostasy grieved the Spirit of God.

My parents did not know where I was, but my mom was praying that the LORD would bring me home. One day, while I was getting knocked around with a sawed-off shotgun in my face, a can of fuel was knocked onto a heater, and a ball of flame engulfed my left side. Today, I greatly appreciate the parallels between the physical fire, which saved my life, and my God, the all-consuming fire, who saved my life.

I was airlifted to a hospital one hour away, and as it would turn out, my parents were already there. My dad had gotten into a terrible accident hours earlier after drinking heavily, and he had also been airlifted to the same hospital. He was now in a coma. The nurse asked my mom, "Do you have a daughter named Amy?" They proceeded to tell her that I was upstairs in the burn unit. My mom collapsed to the floor. As she prayed for a reuniting of our family, this was not what she had anticipated.

I was discharged after skin grafting and a couple of weeks in the hospital, and my dad did come out of his coma. I asked my parents if I could return home, and they welcomed me. My return lasted one month. Then back out I went, desperate to be high. This time, I became pregnant. After several months of continued abuse despite this new circumstance and the complete inability to stay off drugs, I did wind up back at home. By the grace of God, I was able to stay clean. God, and God alone, gets all the credit for this amazing feat. Regrettably, I did not honor him as God or give thanks to Him. If anything, I accredited my strong will and determination in addition to my daughter's presence and the fact that another life now depended upon mine. My world revolved around her.

As my daughter grew, I began to feel the urge to get her into church, and I said another prayer asking God to forgive me. It was a good start, but it never went beyond that. I said a prayer and then proceeded to check off a list of things I thought Christians were supposed to do such as go to church a couple times per week, participate in a Bible study now and again, try to do nice things for people, and live as a productive member of society. THE ONLY THING THAT MATTERS WAS MISSING! An intimate relationship with God Almighty should be the result of our salvation. I had substituted religious activity for a relationship with Jesus Christ, but there is no substitute.

As it is written, I honored God with my lips, but my heart was far from Him. I had failed to completely surrender my will to His will, and I did not know His Word because it did not mean anything to me. If only I had set my face to seek the LORD with all my heart at that time, digging in His Word and desiring to know Him more. I now know there is nothing more beautiful or comforting than hearing the voice of God speak to you through His Word. He uses His Word to correct, convict, direct, lead, encourage, and comfort in a way no one else can. As a child, the Word fell on rocky soil. In my 20s, the Word fell among thorns, and the cares/pleasures of this world and the deceitfulness of riches grew up and choked it (see Matthew 13:7).

When my daughter was approximately 6 years old, I married her father. I wanted her to have a "complete" family so desperately that I ignored all the warnings God revealed. I should have been teaching her that a relationship with Jesus Christ is the only thing that makes us whole, but you cannot effectively teach that which you do not know for yourself. Out of this marriage, my second daughter and my first son were born. The marriage fell apart immediately as old abusive patterns emerged. We had to leave. Marriage counseling did not produce any significant changes, so I filed a legal separation on the grounds that divorce was not acceptable in the eyes of God. My husband then changed it to a divorce, and this took three long years. Finally, it was over, and the court ruled in my favor. I was given sole legal and physical custody. This was nothing but the grace of God; yet, again, I honored Him with my lips while my heart was far from Him.

I resolved to stay single, at least until my three precious children were grown. However, anything done in our own so-called strength is fleeting. One year after the divorce, I was still not seeking God with all my heart and soul. All it took was the right guy to give me some attention, and all that resolve went right out the window.

I was keenly aware of what the Bible had to say about being yoked to an unbeliever as well as remarriage after divorce because I had searched out this knowledge during my divorce. It is written: And He said to them, "Whoever divorces his wife and marries another commits adultery against her, and if she divorces her husband and marries another, she commits adultery" (Mark 10:11-12). You can find it also in Matthew 19:9, Luke 16:18, and Matthew 5:32. I know this is not popular language in today's culture, but it is the Word of God. He can and does redeem our sin and is able to turn it into something beautiful. I know this is the case for many. Praise be to the LORD, for He can bring beauty out of the ashes. However, sin is still sin, and we must call it what it is – Adultery.

In addition to this, I did not want to drag my children through anything else that might cause them pain. However, when you are not in tune to the Holy Spirit, or rather busy tuning Him out, your flesh will win every time. An unbelievable number of warnings came with this relationship. They were warnings of a different nature, but I was being warned by God, nonetheless. With a stubborn heart and a stiff neck, I quenched the Holy Spirit and stepped into a marriage that would take me down in a way I never would have dreamed possible.

Immediately, I knew I screwed up big time, and I wanted to get it annulled. However, I became pregnant on our honeymoon, and our precious twin boys were on their way. I was deeply depressed in this marriage and completely overwhelmed. Even though I loathed alcohol, it was easy to start drinking by the time my twin boys were 3 months old. It was the socially acceptable escape route, even among some Christian circles, so why not? At first, it was just on the weekends, but it did not take long to escalate.

After we put our children to bed, we would drink, and many nights we would fight. I would wake up hung over and miserable, counting down the hours until bedtime when we could begin the madness all over again. Proverbs 23 has something to say about this very thing. Who has woe? Who has sorrow? Who has strife? Who has complaining? Who has wounds without cause? Who has redness of eyes? Those who tarry long over wine, those who go to try mixed wine (or in my case, straight whiskey). Do not look at the wine when it is red, when it sparkles in the cup and goes down smoothly. In the end, it bites like a serpent and stings like an adder. Your eyes will see strange things and your heart utter perverse things. They struck me, you will say, but I was not hurt. They beat me but I did not feel it. When shall I awake? I must have another drink.

It seemed hypocritical to go to church now, so I stopped going altogether. My morals were slipping, and I was now watching, playing, listening to, and saying things I never would have in over a decade of sobriety. In addition, I was now allowing my children to take in content I never would have previously. I was aware of the slipping, and I hated it, but I felt powerless against it, so I tried to justify all of it in my mind. Six to eight months into this new horrid cycle of living, the blackouts began, and each day I woke up completely unable to recall even one minute of the night before. It was a horrific feeling to have zero recollection . . . horrific.

Meanwhile, my oldest daughter, who was 14 years old at the time, was slipping into depression. Although I saw it, I felt completely helpless to help her as I faced my own deep, dark depression. I loathed alcohol now more than I ever had, but I could not stop. I despised feeling controlled by this thing that made me lose all control, and yet . . .

In addition to all of this, we got the news that mom was going to die. She was diagnosed with stage IV pancreatic cancer that had metastasized to her liver. This was devastating. At this point in my life, I loved my mom dearly. She always had my back, and she played a huge role in the lives of my children. She was also their only real source of spiritual guidance, so this sent me deeper into the pit of despair. It was estimated she had six weeks to live, but she underwent alternative treatments and stuck around for nine months. Then, the LORD took her home.

After she was gone, it was business as usual, now with an extra layer of grief. Still trying to escape, we were still getting drunk at night and still fighting. One dreadful night, eight months after mom had gone home to be with the LORD, my sister came downstairs to our apartment during one of our fights. I do not remember any of this, but at some point, my anger turned from my husband and onto my sister, and I assaulted her. She woke my two sleeping children, put all five of them into my van, and drove away. I was completely blacked out through it all. The very first memory I have from that night is frantically running up my driveway, chasing my van full of my children, and yelling for my sister to come back.

Two days later, my sister and a friend of mine showed up to the house, not with my children, as I had anticipated, but with paperwork stating they had gotten temporary guardianship of my children. I was in shock and completely devastated. I had to excuse myself to scream and cry. The reason for it, they said, was to enable me to get help for my alcoholism via a one-year treatment program. The thought of being separated from my children for an entire year was an excruciating and unbearable thought, so I did not immediately agree to this. They told me there was no use fighting the guardianship because I did not have money for a lawyer, and they were certain I would lose.

In the days following, I was bullied into conceding. They claimed it was the only way they would allow me to see my children. By day three of being without them, I was losing my mind; I desperately needed to see my children. Through gut-wrenching tears, I signed this horrible paperwork, feeling completely helpless and totally hopeless. They would not let me speak with them on the phone, but I did get to see them several times that week. However, that would change drastically. With each passing week, I was allowed less and less time with them as the guardians told me their schedules were far too busy. It got to the point where I was only allowed to see them for one hour every other week. Children's services was not involved, but in hindsight, I would have done well to get them involved. Nevertheless, God is sovereign.

Several months into this mess, as I grieved the absence of my children and the extreme lack of visitation with them, I incurred a couple of DUI's. When my sister caught wind of this, I received a text from her which said, "Due to your recent circumstances, you may not have any visitation until further notice." This crushed me in every way. It completely devastated me to my core. I had never felt so helpless in my entire life. Never.

A passage from Isaiah 47 had become my reality. Now, therefore, hear this you lover of pleasures, who sit securely and say in your heart, I shall not sit as a widow or know the loss of children. These two things shall come to you in a moment, in one day, the loss of children and widowhood shall come upon you in full measure in spite of your many sorceries and the great power of your enchantments. You felt secure in your wickedness. You said, no one sees me. Your wisdom and your knowledge led you astray, and you said in your heart I am, and there is no one besides me, but evil shall come upon you which you will not know how to charm away. Disaster shall fall upon you for which you will not be able to atone, and ruin shall come upon you suddenly of which you know nothing.

While the choices made by the guardians of my children were completely unacceptable and not at all just, God was meticulously orchestrating all of this in order to get my attention and bring me to repentance. He was stripping me of my many idolatries and false identities, so I would find my identity in Him alone. I have completely forgiven the injustices that occurred, and I know and understand they were acting on behalf of the LORD, whether they were aware of it or not. I pray that God has given them the ability to forgive me as well.

There are no words in any language that could adequately describe the depth of my sorrow and the intense devastation in my soul over this separation from my children – No words. It was and continues to be the most intensely painful emotion I have ever experienced. I have never felt so utterly and completely helpless, and as a mother who deeply loves her children (self-destructing as I was), it nearly destroyed me.

My worst fear was being separated from my children via some horrible circumstance such as kidnapping. God Almighty has this to say in Isaiah 66. These have chosen their own ways, and their soul delights in their abominations. I also will choose harsh treatment for them and bring their fears upon them because when I called, no one answered. When I spoke, they did not listen, but they did what was evil in my eyes and chose that in which I did not delight. Hear the Word of the LORD you who tremble at His Word.

The house was eerily quiet, and for the first time in almost fifteen years, there were no needs to be met, and there was no one for whom I could care. Needless to say, I did not want to be there. Lacking gas money to just drive, I would go sit in various parking lots and cry and cry and cry. Yet, even in all that intense sorrow, I still did not surrender to the LORD! In fact, going back to drugs became my new route of escape, a familiar false god/idol of the past. If I was a mess before, I was really a mess now. For if after they have escaped the defilements of the world through the knowledge of our Lord and Savior Jesus Christ, they are again entangled in them and overcome, the last state has become worse for them than the first, for it would have been better for them never to have known the way of righteousness than after knowing it to turn back from the holy commandment delivered to them. What the true proverb says has happened to them: The dog returns to its own vomit, and the sow after washing herself returns to wallow in the mire (2 Peter 2:20-22).

In a short time, many difficult and twisted things took place, and I met people I wish I never had. In addition, I got five DUI's in a two-month period. Like dominoes, after losing my mom and my children, I lost my car, my license, my income, and my house, including all my things, all of my many sentimental things. Furthermore, what very little I managed to reaccumulate kept getting stolen. The LORD was attempting to get me to come to the end of myself. He had stripped me of all false identities. I could no longer find my worth in titles like mother, wife, or daughter, and now he was stripping me of my false sense of security in possessions and money. For the first time in my life, I had absolutely nothing and no one, and it was as if I had stepped into some ultra-demented twilight zone.

I went to rehab for a month and found out about a one-year program, so that became the next goal. I left the area in an attempt to get myself together, and I was now beginning to talk to God, sincerely. I was not trying to conjure up a prayer full of so-called Christian words and phrases as I had done sparingly in the past, but I was sincerely talking to Him from my heart. It felt like the start of something new and exciting. He even did something sweet for me in response to something I said to Him. It totally blew my mind. He was showing me that He loved me and that He would take care of me. I even recounted the story to others in my amazement.

Then . . . I met a guy . . . sigh. This is where Acts 3:14 became my reality. You denied the Holy and Righteous One and asked for a murderer to be granted to you (yes, a literal murderer). I rejected my God, who saves me from all my calamities and my distresses and said to Him, set a king over me (I Samuel 10:19). Against all my better judgment and every prompting of the Holy Spirit, I gave into this relationship.

So, what was the allure of this man? He had a proven history of showing himself to be a warrior. After being separated from my children and really everything I had ever known, the LORD began to open my eyes to many things. He began to reveal evidence of things to come *much sooner* than I had previously imagined, such as the disarming of civilians, one-world government, one-world currency, and the mark of the beast, to name a few. I could see horrific trouble coming very soon. I thought, if only I could strengthen myself and take on the mentality of a warrior, I would endure more successfully until my end. Of course, this was not right thinking. I should have been throwing myself on the mercy of the LORD, not relying on mine or others' so-called strength. It was yet another foolish and futile move. I was seeking training and protection in man and not in God. In addition, this guy listened to me spill out my woes, and in this I found satisfaction. I should have been seeking my God, casting all my anxieties on Him because He cares for me. As spoken through the prophet Jeremiah, cursed is the one who trusts in man and makes flesh his strength, whose heart turns away from the LORD. They are like a shrub in the desert and will not see any good come.

This guy would turn out to be deeply disturbed. He was a serial killer with a sexual perversion unlike anything I had ever known. He would also become the father of my third daughter and my fourth son. This time in my life would bring me to a whole new level of demented twilight zone. It was next level evil, whether from this guy or his associates. Though I do not wish to go into detail, let me assure you, it was insane. It was, in fact, so insane that if I were to write about my experiences, you would probably not believe me. I will say this; thrust into the depths of darkness which surrounded me, sin lost its allure, and I felt completely repulsed by all of it.

I did complete a one-year program, but it took closer to two years. I did not know my sister's new address, but throughout these years, I sent gifts and cards for my children to the church we used to attend. I was never able to talk with them on the phone since I had lost my phone and all my phone numbers, but once I completed the program, I began attempting to contact my sister via letter. I was so excited to come up with a plan to reconcile with my children. It had been a desperate desire for so long. However, I was then informed that she had filed for adoption. This was a crushing blow. I was so excited about reconciling with my precious, beloved children, but instead, more devastation was added to my longing. God would later show me this scripture in Luke 13:34b-35. How often would I have gathered your children together as a hen gathers her brood under her wings, and you were not willing! Behold, your house is forsaken. And I tell you, you will not see me until you say, "Blessed is He who comes in the name of the LORD!" My rebellion and refusal to submit myself to God caused so much heartache for me, for my children, and for God himself. Obedience matters.

I did attempt to fight the adoption, but I was in way over my head with the evil that encompassed me. On the train ride over to the adoption hearing, I knew in my heart that God was telling me to concede. I wrestled heavily with that idea, but I knew it would ultimately be best for them. As I said, I was in way over my head at this point, and I had no desire to drag them into any of it.

After voicing my decision to my lawyer, with a shaky hand and many more gut-wrenching tears, I signed the papers. I left that courthouse completely heartbroken. Again, there are no words to adequately describe the devastation. I was shattered. Then, something happened. A song began to play on my phone, and I knew it was by God's sovereignty. The song was "Need You Now" by Plumb, and I cried out to God, and I truly felt His gentle comfort. How many nights I spent sobbing on my bed so hard I could barely breathe, leading up to this fateful day full of sorrow and tears. The LORD gave, and the LORD has taken away. Blessed be the name of the LORD. The pain of missing your children *never* goes away, but as I unceasingly lift them up in prayer, I am so grateful my God is a healer, and nothing is too hard for Him!

At this point, the threats and actions of this disturbed individual were growing in intensity, but God! God Almighty protected us and kept me informed and abreast of all that was going on. I will refrain from identifying the horrendous things done by him, for it is shameful even to speak of the things that they do in secret (Ephesians 5:12), but please understand that horrifying does not even begin to adequately portray.

I loathed and grieved over the dreadful sins of this man but, strangely, I found myself feeling sorrow for him and for what he had endured, which led to his own hardness of heart. I could not explain it, but God was beginning to reveal deep spiritual truths to me, which I was now starting to grasp on a whole new level. It was through this relationship I learned of God's deep and unconditional love for me and the undeserved forgiveness of my sin. God gave me an unmerited love for this man despite his heinous crimes, so that I would know and understand God's unmerited love for me despite my heinous crimes against Him (God). Do not misunderstand me. The crimes were absolutely repulsive, and I did not want to be within a mile of this man. By this point, we did not live together and, indeed, I kept my distance.

Interestingly, the LORD was now using many of my encounters with other people to reveal to me the depth of my own sin. An injustice would take place or a situation that bothered me would occur, and the Holy Spirit would say, remember when you _____, and He would remind me of a time I did that very thing or something similar, either directly or indirectly. This included strange, forgotten memories that went back as far as childhood. He also showed me that the intense betrayal I encountered from my family and friends, which completely crushed me, did not hold a candle to my own intense betrayal of my God and my Savior. I had the same experience as the woman of Samaria, seen in John Ch. 4, who exclaimed, "He told me all that I ever did."

I was beginning to realize my sin and betrayal for what it is – A personal offense to my Lord and Savior. There was a humbling taking place, and the layers of pride were being peeled back, revealing my true human vulnerability and frailty. My skewed and darkened perspective was beginning to clear up, and by God's grace, I was beginning to see things the way He sees them. Yet, I was still not fully surrendered. I was still grasping at some semblance of control, even though it had been obvious for years that I was definitely not the one in control.

The intense threats from this man began increasing in severity. He started killing again, and I knew we were next. One particularly fearful night, as a threat arose, the LORD impressed upon me to change into all black clothes and get out of the apartment. My children slept in their stroller as I walked. I then noticed we were being followed by a vehicle. We came upon a wide-open space. In the middle of this huge empty lot sat a dumpster casting a lone shadow. Loud and clear, the LORD said through my spirit, run to the shadow! I did not hesitate; I took off running. As soon as we were out of sight, hidden in the shadow, the car that had been following us drove by. The beauty of being safely hidden in the shadow would come to mean a great deal to me and became a recurring theme in my life. For he who dwells in the shelter of the Most High will abide in the shadow of the Almighty. The LORD God was saying, run to the shadow, my dear daughter, run to me! I just did not fully realize it yet. You, O God, have been my help, and in the shadow of your wings, I will sing for joy. My soul clings to you; your right hand upholds me (Psalm 63:7-8).

Not too long after this episode came a night that would change the course of my life. As the dark set in, a threat emerged. Having been forced to leave my apartment for safety in the middle of the night several times by now, I was sick of it and did not wish to do it again. Instead, I simply said, "LORD, I am tired, and I am sick of fleeing to survive. If you allow us to be blown up, hurt, or killed, so be it, but I do not want to spend one more night walking outside again. You can protect us if you want to." I laid down beside my sleeping children. They had their own beds, but I kept them close just in case there was a chance to scoop them up and get out quickly should danger strike. I did not own a Bible, but I took out my phone and began to look up various Psalms. I read aloud in an effort to connect with God and find some peace, and I began to pour out my heart to Him.

I felt so desperate and so fearful. I knew God was, in fact, my only hope, if I had any hope at all. Since He had been revealing the extent of my sin to me, telling me everything I ever did, I realized I needed repentance. I had strayed a very long way, indeed, and I was finally coming to my senses. Through many tears, I poured out my heart to Him and begged for the mercy only He could give me. Thankfully, while I was still a long way off, my Father saw me and felt compassion. He ran to embrace me, and He kissed me (Luke 15 – The Prodigal Son). He burst the bonds of sin and oppression and set me free from the darkness, which had manifested itself in the physical realm.

In my spirit, I heard Him say, look up at me. I looked up and out my window into the heavens, and I began to worship in song. "Turn your eyes upon Jesus. Look full in His wonderful face, and the things of earth will grow strangely dim in the light of His glory and grace," penned by Helen Lemmel, 1922. The enemy tried so hard to distract me with fear, but by the grace of God, I was able to keep my eyes (physical and spiritual) firmly fixed on the glory revealed to me. The presence of God was beautiful and overwhelming. He felt so near to me; it literally felt as if I could reach out and touch Him. It was truly unlike anything I had ever known, and as I fixed my eyes on Jesus that night, the things of earth did, in fact, grow strangely dim. I had never known the depth of that kind of love and intimacy with the LORD my God, but it was definitely the beginning of something truly amazing – A real relationship.

It all began with massive affliction followed by true humility and total surrender. Opening my heart to Him, I admitted, "LORD, I need you. I am nothing without you. I have no hope without you. I desperately need you." Thankfully, his thoughts are not our thoughts, and his ways are higher than our ways, so He joyfully forgave me and threw a celebration.

Like the Prodigal Son, I also asked that my inheritance be given to me early (at age 7). I then proceeded to squander said inheritance on reckless living. After being humbled, I finally came to my senses and sought His mercy. He responded by running to embrace me in His compassion. He covered me in His best robe (the righteousness of Jesus Christ), and He threw a celebration saying, this my child was dead and is alive again. She was lost but is found, and they began to celebrate. It is truly beautiful imagery once you get past longing for pig slop and come to your senses.

If you find yourself at a difficult stage in your life, living in disobedience and wishing for pig slop, I implore you, on behalf of Christ, to be reconciled to God, your Father. He is standing on the doorstep, watching and waiting for you to come home, so he can cover you with compassionate forgiveness. We serve an Awesome God who desires restoration! Do not delay.

After this amazing encounter with our Creator, I found the next several days to be totally weird, for lack of a better word. I realized in every fiber of my being that this world was not my home, and it felt completely foreign. My heart and mind were now set on God, my treasure in Heaven. However, I also became keenly aware that I must be here; God had work for me to accomplish. With my pride finally out of the way, He could now use this once useless vessel. Do not misunderstand me; we will fight the sin of pride until the day we enter the Eternal, so as we pray without ceasing, we must keep the request for humility ever before us. Again, it is God who gives us our abilities. Apart from Him, we can do nothing. The LORD spoke to my heart in those days telling me that I was, indeed, a warrior but of a different variety than I had envisioned. He was calling me to be a prayer warrior, and so I received my first assignment.

One week following this total surrender, my children and I had to flee for refuge. Seething in the face of this renewed covenant with my God, the enemy would attempt to take me out once more. Indeed, this attack would fail. I leaned into the LORD even more, and He told me to run for my life. It was through this act of obedience I would embark upon a spiritual journey that would transform me in ways I never dreamed possible.

I want to say it again. Obedience matters. Do not listen to the words of the prophets who prophesy to you filling you with vain hopes. They say continually to those who despise the Word of the LORD, it shall be well with you; and to everyone who stubbornly follows his own heart, they say no disaster shall come upon you (Jeremiah 23:16-17). You have wearied the LORD with your words . . . by saying everyone who does evil is good in the sight of the LORD and He delights in them (Malachi 2:17). If you will not take it to heart to give honor to my Name, says the LORD of Hosts, then I will send the curse upon you, and I will curse your blessings. Indeed, I have already cursed them because you do not lay it to heart (Malachi 2:2).

Blessings and curses remain consequences today for obedience and disobedience. Idolatry was forbidden then just as it is forbidden now, and most of our disobedience, if not all of it, has its roots in idolatry. The first and most significant commandment is to have no other gods besides the One True Living God, yet we fail so miserably to keep it. More to come about what I have learned about idolatry later in this book. If you do not believe that curses are still a consequence for disobedience, please allow me to share some scripture with you.

But if you will not obey the voice of the LORD your God or be careful to do all His commandments and statutes, I command you today, then all these curses shall come upon you and overtake you. Cursed shall you be in the city and cursed shall you be in the field . . . The LORD will send on you curses, confusion, and frustration in all that you undertake to do until you are destroyed on account of the evil of your deeds because you have forsaken me . . . You shall be only oppressed and robbed continually, and there shall be no one to help you . . . You shall build a house, but you shall not dwell in it . . . your sons and your daughters shall be given to another people while your eyes look on and fail with longing for them all day long, but you shall be helpless . . . You shall be only oppressed and crushed continually, so that you are driven mad by the sights that your eyes see . . . The LORD will bring you and your king whom you set over you to a nation neither you nor your fathers have known . . . You shall become a horror, a proverb, and a byword among all the peoples where the LORD will lead you away. You shall carry much seed into the field and shall gather in little . . . You shall birth sons and daughters, but they shall not be yours, for they shall go into captivity . . . because you did not obey the voice of the LORD . . . There will be no resting place for the sole of your foot, but the LORD will give you there a trembling heart and failing eyes and a languishing soul. Your life shall hang in doubt before you. Night and day, you shall be in dread and have no assurance of your life. In the morning, you will say, if only it were evening! And at evening you shall say if only it were morning because of the dread that your heart shall feel and the sights that your eyes shall see (see Deuteronomy 28). This scripture, *word for word*, describes my life experience like a script.

Gratefully, we see in Deuteronomy 30, God's merciful restoration . . . And when all these things come upon you, the blessing and the curse, which I have set before you, and you call them to mind among all the nations where I have driven you and return to the LORD your God, you and your children, and obey His voice in all I command you today with all your heart and with all your soul, then the LORD your God will restore your fortunes and have mercy on you, and He will gather you from where He scattered you . . . And the LORD your God will circumcise your heart and the heart of your offspring, so that you will love the LORD your God with all your heart and with all your soul, that you may live . . . And you shall again obey the voice of the LORD.

God is not mocked; we will reap what we sow. Living a life of disobedience led to the reaping of curses and destruction, which not only affected me but those around me. The LORD had not disowned me for He will never leave you nor forsake you, but He will discipline you in just measure until you wake up to the truth.

Agree with God, and be at peace; thereby, good will come to you (Job 22:21). Agree that what He calls evil is, in fact, evil and that what He calls good is good. Abhor what He abhors. Love what He loves. In a day and age when evil is called good and now good is called evil, you must know the Word for yourselves. If you do not know God's truth,

His Word through and through, you will be led astray. It is not a matter of if; it is a matter of how far. God spoke to me in my prosperity, but I said, I will not listen. This had been my way from my youth, that I had not obeyed His voice (Jeremiah 22:21-22). Are you living a life of disobedience? Repent! Repent and return to the LORD your God. Obedience matters.

Praise the LORD that he comforts His people and will have compassion on His afflicted. He does not grieve the children of man or afflict them from His heart (Lamentations 3:33). The goal is always restoration. Behold, it was for my welfare that I had great bitterness, but in love you have delivered my life from the pit of destruction for you have cast all my sins behind your back (Isaiah 38:17). For a brief moment, I deserted you, but with great compassion, I will gather you. In overflowing anger for a moment, I hid my face from you, but with everlasting love, I will have compassion on you, says the LORD, your Redeemer (Isaiah 54:7-8).

There is a deceptive idea circulating today that because we are under the new and better covenant through the precious blood of Christ, the Old Testament is now irrelevant. Nothing could be further from the truth. It is true that animal sacrifice has become obsolete because Jesus Christ was the once for all Lamb of God who takes away the sins of the world. The Old Testament, however, is far from obsolete in these days. First and foremost, the entire Old Testament points forward to Jesus Christ which, in and of itself, makes it indisputably relevant. Furthermore, I hope the few (of many) examples provided from my own life demonstrate how the Old Testament remains living and active along with the New Testament. Unfortunately, "Yes, to this day whenever Moses is read a veil lies over their hearts" (II Corinthians 3:15).

In Matthew 5:17-18, Jesus says something remarkable. Do not think that I have come to abolish the Law or the Prophets. I have not come to abolish them but to fulfill them. For truly I say to you, until heaven and earth pass away, not an iota, not a dot will pass from the Law until all is accomplished. Verse 19 goes on to say, whoever relaxes one of the least of these commandments and teaches others to do the same will be called least in the kingdom of heaven. In fact, if one turns away his ear from hearing the law, even his prayer is an abomination (Proverbs 28:9).

One verse that is widely used out of context and twisted to our own harm is Romans 7:6. Certainly, I used this in my own life to justify my own lack of obedience. It says, but now we are released from the Law, having died to that which held us captive, so that we serve in the new way of the spirit and not in the old way of the written code.

We are, indeed, released from the sentence of death for failure to keep the whole Law, which none of us can do. We have instead received the perfect obedience and righteousness of our Lord and Savior, Jesus Christ, if we have been born again and given His Spirit as a guarantee. We have not, however, been released from obedience to the Law. Rather, we are released from the death sentence incurred when we fail to keep it. Given by God himself, the Law is holy, and the commandment holy, and just, and good (Romans 7:12 KJV).

Another verse that seems to be commonly misused is Romans 10:9. Because, if you confess with your mouth that Jesus is Lord and believe in your heart that God raised him from the dead, you will be saved. The misconception arises out of that phrase "confess with your mouth that Jesus is Lord," because this is deeper than an act of speaking. What is a Lord? By definition, it is someone who has power, authority, and influence; a master or ruler. If I declare Jesus is Lord, then I declare He has the power and authority. He is master and ruler, and I have chosen obedience and submission to Him. If I just say with my mouth, "Jesus is Lord," but I do not submit to Him or obey Him, then, in reality, I have not actually made him Lord of my life. We see this come out in Jesus Christ's own words when He says, "Why do you call me 'Lord, Lord,' and not do what I tell you?" (Luke 6:46). Or how about when He says, "Not everyone who says to me, 'Lord, Lord,' will enter the kingdom of heaven, but the one who does the will of my Father who is in heaven" (Matthew 7:21).

The Law of the LORD is perfect, reviving the soul. The testimony of the LORD is sure, making wise the simple. The precepts of the LORD are right, rejoicing the heart. The commandment of the LORD is pure, enlightening the eyes. The fear of the LORD is clean, enduring forever. The rules (decrees) of the LORD are true and righteous altogether. More to be desired are they than gold, even much fine gold, sweeter also than honey and drippings of the honeycomb. Moreover, by them is your servant warned. In keeping them, there is great reward (Psalm 19:7-11). In addition, Psalm 119 is the longest chapter in all of God's Word devoted solely to the perfect Law of God.

Our obedience matters to God, and it should matter to us, not merely because we will be disciplined for our disobedience. No! We should obey out of love and reverence and a fear of the LORD. As we enjoy intimate fellowship with our faithful Creator, we will desire to be faithful in return.

The greatest commandment is to love the LORD your God with all your heart, mind, soul, and strength. Practically speaking, what might that look like? As it is written in the scriptures, our obedience is the action behind our love for Him. If you love me, you will keep my commandments (John 14:15). You are my friends if you do what I command you (John 15:14). Whoever has my commandments and keeps them, he it is who loves me (John 14:21). And by this we know if we have come to know Him, if we keep His commandments (I John 2:3).

It is important to note that obedience from the whole heart and an outward show of obedience are two very different things. You can clean the outside of the "cup" and inside be full of all manner of unrighteousness, like a Pharisee (hypocrite). This is the route I went in my 20s. I was not a pharisaical rule follower, per se, but I attempted to clean up the outside while inside I remained full of self-indulgence, hypocrisy, and lawlessness.

We also must be on alert that we are not obeying *so that* we will receive favor from the LORD. To the contrary, if we are in Christ, we have already received *all* of His favor. We cannot earn any more love from Him. He already loves us perfectly. Obedience, rather, should be our response to His perfect love for us. The more intimate and personal our relationship with our God, the more awe we have for Him. The more awe and reverence we have for Him, the more our desires will line up with His desires. We will want to do the things we know are pleasing to Him and abstain from the things which are not.

Obedience matters to God and it, therefore, should matter to us. Disobedience to the voice of God will not redact our salvation if, indeed, we have received salvation, but it will break our fellowship with Him. God is light, and in Him is no darkness at all. If we say we have fellowship with Him while we walk in darkness, we lie and do not practice the truth (I John 1:5-6).

Indeed, we will continue to sin as long as we are in these bodies of flesh, until the imperfect is made perfect, until the mortal puts on immortality. However, when the LORD does reveal our sin, we must repent quickly and submit once again to His Spirit. Be careful that you do not stiffen your neck and act in the stubbornness of your heart when you have clearly been given direction, a nudge, or a command from the LORD. Sanctification (being set apart and being made holy/becoming more like Christ) is a process, and the transformation is ever ongoing.

How do we become more like Jesus Christ? By becoming one with Jesus Christ. When we allow His nature to become our nature by truly surrendering our own stubborn will, we find that it will, indeed, cost us. It will cost us the things of this world. It is an amazing trade – the things of this world for oneness with Christ – but it will wage war with your flesh and your mind. You must be prepared for this by clinging to Christ and to God's Word.

I entreat you – Read your Bible, cover to cover, again and again and again! Have you read it once? Read it again. Have you read it 100 times? Read it again. You cannot and will not ever get to the bottom of it. It is living and active, but only if you read it! If you are physically unable to read it, try listening to it on audio, but if you are able . . . read it.

Devotions are of some value. There are seasons wherein I start my day with several of them, but they are no substitute for reading the Word of God, of which I also read several chapters. There are other seasons when it is simply me and God's Word. Sermons are of some value. I really enjoy and can get much out of a good word from the LORD through a preacher of His Word, but it is no substitute for reading the Word of God yourself. A well-written book regarding the things of God is of some value, but it is no substitute for reading the Word of God. If you do not crave the Word of God in your life, something has gone awry and you are at risk of losing your stability. In that case, pray! Pour out your heart to God. Do you need to seek forgiveness? Do it. Do you need to surrender your will? Do it. That is where it begins.

Maybe you find yourself in a season that feels a little bit dry and you are just not all that interested. Tell Him and ask Him to help you. When He does, do not quench His Spirit but heed His voice. The more we quench the voice of God, the less we hear the voice of God, until one day you have drifted so far from your relationship with Him that you will hear His voice no more. Therefore, we must pay much closer attention to what we have heard lest we drift away from it (Hebrews 2:1). Read His Word and strive to obey His Word, continually praying and asking God to give you the ability to do so. For I know that nothing good dwells in me, that is in my flesh, for I have the desire to do what is right but not the ability to carry it out (Romans 7:18).

Surrender is where it all begins, but we must choose daily to submit our will to His. It is not a one and done deal. It is a choice that we make from the first moment of the day to the last moment of the day and every moment in between. Take up your cross daily, saying to the Father, not my will but yours be done, just as we were taught by our Savior.

What is important in any act of obedience is the posture of your heart before God Almighty. When you hear that still, small voice or feel that nudge in a particular direction, will you submit or will you go your own way, somehow justifying your decision? It is not hard to choose this latter path of destruction. He will often ask us to do something we do not want to do or He will ask us to stop doing something we want to keep doing. I cannot think of a time when it has been super easy for me to obey. Obedience is not easy, but it is totally worth it.

Sometimes our obedience will not make any sense from a natural perspective. Sometimes the orders given might seem downright insane. Then I wonder how crazy the Israelites must have felt (or seemed in the eyes of others) as they marched around Jericho or how Gideon's teeny tiny army felt wielding lanterns. Because God can see all that we cannot even fathom, our actions done in obedience may not be widely accepted by others, and we need to be okay with that. We must dare to be different. We must shed our need for approval and the fear of missing out and replace it with a true fear of the LORD. You can be confident that everything our Father asks of us is in our best interest. Keep this in mind; he who is faithful in little will be given much more.

I would like to take a moment to speak on one of the commands God put on my heart to obey. As I read through God's Word again and again and again, I could not ignore how much ink is given to the honoring of the Sabbath. I discerned in my heart that it was the LORD's desire for me to honor the Sabbath day and keep it holy, and so I have. I would like to take a moment to address Colossians 2:16 (KJV), which states the following: Let no man therefore judge you in meat, or in drink, or in respect of an holyday, or of the new moon, or of the sabbath days. The term "sabbath days" is referring not to *the* Sabbath day but to those special days that were also known as sabbath days such as Feast of Unleavened Bread, Day of Atonement, etc. There were false teachers at that time claiming Jewish ceremonies as essential for spiritual advancement, which is not a position that I take. However, when it comes to *the* Sabbath day, which was first instituted at creation and reinstituted through the ten commandments, it remains a commandment from God for us today.

I have heard people state that because the Law was given to the Jews, it does not apply to us (gentiles). However, we (gentiles) have been grafted in. We are circumcised in heart and heirs of the promise along with Abraham's blood descendants. We have been grafted into the family tree of God's chosen people, so do not let the fact that you have not been born of Jewish descent deter you from obedience to God's Law. Let not the foreigner who has joined himself to the LORD say the LORD will surely separate me from His people (Isaiah 56:3). Of course, He will not. You shall have one statute, both for the sojourner and the native (Numbers 9:14 and others).

- In Genesis 2:2-3, we are told that on the seventh day God finished His work that He had done, and He rested on the seventh day from all His work that He had done. So God blessed the seventh day and made it holy, because on it God rested from all His work that He had done in creation.
- In Exodus 20:8-11, it is number four of ten commandments written in stone by the finger of God, which states, remember the Sabbath day and keep it holy.

- In Exodus 31:12-18, the LORD said, above all, you shall keep my Sabbaths.

- It shows up again in Deuteronomy 5:12-15 under the ten commandments with the addition that we should remember that we were slaves in the land of Egypt and brought out with a mighty hand and an outstretched arm; therefore, the LORD your God commanded you to keep the Sabbath day. If you are a believer, you too have been rescued and brought out from Egypt, redeemed by a mighty hand and the outstretched arms of Jesus Christ.

- In Nehemiah 13:15-22, we see the people are committing evil by profaning the Sabbath, treading winepresses and buying and selling, and Nehemiah attempts to bring reform.

- In Isaiah 56:2, it says, blessed is the man who does this . . . who keeps my Sabbath, not profaning it and keeps his hand from doing any evil. Verses 4-8 go on to talk about the blessing for everyone who keeps the Sabbath, not profaning it.

- In Ezekiel 20:12, God says, I gave them my Sabbaths as a sign between me and them that they might know that I am the LORD who sanctifies them. Then in verse 16, it says, they rejected my rules and did not walk in my statutes and profaned my Sabbaths for their heart went after their idols.

- In Ezekiel 22:26, it says, they have made no distinction between the holy and the common, neither have they taught the difference between the unclean and the clean, and they have disregarded my Sabbaths, so that I am profaned among them.

- In Matthew 24:20, we see Jesus proclaim we ought to pray our flight not be in winter or on a Sabbath.

- In Luke 4:16, Jesus went to the synagogue on the Sabbath day, and He stood up to read.
- In Luke 23:56, the disciples rested on the Sabbath day according to the commandment.

In Acts, the disciples are still honoring the Sabbath, and we know from history that the early Christians/church kept the Sabbath. According to Josephus, "There is not any city of the Grecians, nor any of the Barbarians nor any nation whatsoever, whither our custom of resting on the seventh day hath not come!" (M'Clatchie, "Notes and Queries on China and Japan" (edited by Dennys), Vol 4, Nos 7,8, P. 100)

So why do we, as Christians today, seemingly overlook the fourth commandment? We find importance in all the others: Have no other gods, make no idols, do not take God's name in vain, honor your parents, do not murder, do not commit adultery, do not steal, do not bear false witness, do not covet. So why not keep number four and keep the Sabbath day holy? In fact, we see in Isaiah 66:22-23 that from new moon to new moon and from Sabbath to Sabbath, all flesh will worship before the LORD in the new heavens and the new earth, and if we continue reading in Colossians 2:17, these are a shadow of the things to come. If the Sabbath is set to continue into eternity, eternity itself is a Sabbath rest for believers (Hebrews 4:9), and God created the Sabbath as He, himself, rested, why do we think we are above honoring it now?

I learned over the course of my life to place value upon my busyness. Being busy made me feel useful and important as if it added value to my identity. I wonder how many of you have also fallen for this deception. Instead of doing what God has called us to do (what

He modeled for us) and rest, we are busy, distracted, and missing out on a tremendous blessing of rest in the Lord.

Obviously, we fail miserably short of keeping God's commands. Jesus Christ pointed that out as He spoke on murdering your brother in your heart through your hatred of him. Glory be to God for making a way, through the precious blood of Christ, when there was no way, but the commands of the LORD are not to be ignored; they are for our good and His glory.

I have been so blessed through this simple act of obedience to keep the Sabbath day holy and to rest according to the Word of the LORD. I would encourage you to give it a try. Maybe you are thinking, yes, I would like to try honoring the Sabbath, but in practical terms what might that look like today? In response, I would like to share a few more scriptures. In Exodus 35:1-3, it says, keep the Sabbath and kindle no fire in your dwelling place. Nehemiah 10:31 says, and if the people of the land bring in goods or grain on the Sabbath day to sell, we will not buy on a Sabbath day. Jeremiah 17:21-22 says, take care for the sake of your lives and do not bear a burden on the Sabbath day or bring it in by the gates. Do not carry a burden out of your houses or do any work.

According to these few verses, my aim is to have all my cooking done for Saturday on Friday before the sun goes down (I know there are some who believe you can pick any day of the week; however, the Bible is clear that it is to be kept on the seventh day, which is from sundown Friday to sundown Saturday); I do not buy or sell anything; and I refrain from work and bearing a burden outside my home. On the flipside, it is good to spend that time in worship of and seeking the presence of the LORD.

More generally speaking, I like what Isaiah 58:13 has to say: If you turn back your foot from the Sabbath from doing your pleasure (business) on my holy day and call the Sabbath a delight and the holy day of the LORD honorable, if you honor it not going your own ways or seeking your own pleasure (pursuing your own business) or talking idly, then you shall take delight in the LORD.

That is the bottom line, is it not? To lay down our will and our pleasure for His will. He calls us to rest and rest we should; the details are between you and God. It will not always be easy. There are days in which my will to work rises up against my desire to do God's will, and I must pray and worship through the struggle. I have shared my aim as an example, not as a blueprint. I also do not want to imply that I get it right every time. I know I do not, so I ask Him to forgive me and thank Him for paying my penalty.

Jesus said to those who had believed Him, if you abide in my Word, you are truly my disciples, and you will know the truth, and the truth will set you free (John 8:31-32). We must abide (stay) in the Word daily. If we cease to abide in the Word, we will cease to be a disciple. We will cease to be fruitful. We will begin to wander and drift. Just because you know something at one point in your life does not mean you will keep it. Even what you think you have can be taken away (Luke 8:18). If we are abiding in the Word of God, however, the enemy's tactics become much less effective. Abiding in the Word guards us from deception because we are abiding in the Truth. To be clear, when I speak of abiding in His Word, I do not mean inundate yourself with sermons, podcasts, devotionals, etc. First and above all, you must be alone with the Word of God. Through His Holy Spirit, He will interpret it to you.

I love the story in Luke 24 recounting the walk to Emmaus. He (Jesus) interpreted to them (two of his disciples) in all the scriptures the things concerning himself . . . Their eyes were opened . . . Their hearts burned within them while He opened up the scriptures to them . . . He opened their minds to understand the scriptures. God himself will teach His children (Isaiah 54).

I submit that we are always learning and never able to arrive at a knowledge of the truth (II Timothy 3:7) because we are not putting the things we learn into practice through obedience.

Beloved children of God, read God's Word often and strive to be a doer of His Word. However, keep your eyes off of your performance and firmly fixed upon Jesus Christ, your Redeemer. O LORD, you will ordain peace for us, for you have indeed done for us all our works (Isaiah 26:12).

- Because they have rejected the Law of the LORD and have not kept His statutes, their lies have led them astray, those after which their fathers walked (Amos 2:4).
- The friendship (secret counsel) of the LORD is for those who fear Him, and He makes known to them His covenant (Psalm 25:14).
- I will instruct you and teach you in the way you should go. I will counsel you with my eye upon you. Be not like a horse or mule without understanding, which must be curbed with bit and bridle or it will not stay near you (Psalm 32:8-9).
- Cease to hear instruction, my child, and you will stray from the words of knowledge (Proverbs 19:27). He gives knowledge to those who have understanding (Daniel 2:21). The fear of the LORD is the beginning of wisdom and to turn away from evil is understanding (Job 28:28).

CHAPTER TWO

Trust in the LORD

Trust in the LORD with all your heart and lean not on
your own understanding. In all your ways acknowledge
Him, and He will make your paths straight.
Be not wise in your own eyes.
Fear the LORD and turn away from evil.
Proverbs 3:5-7

THE FIRST LESSON I had to learn was true surrender. The next lesson I learned was trusting the LORD with all of my heart. As the LORD led the Israelites out of Egypt through many signs and wonders, so He would lead me and my children out of "Egypt" and into the wilderness where He would guide me, lead me, and faithfully provide for us all along the way.

I arrived home one afternoon to find my apartment had been broken into . . . again. I had that eerie feeling of impending doom you get right before your life is about to be taken. I was terrified, and the danger was imminent. I knew we had to go, and we had to go right now. I asked God, "What should I take?" The response I understood was this: Nothing. Do not take your cellphone; do not take your stroller (on which I had found a tracking device welded); and do not worry about what you will eat, drink, or wear. Believe me when I say

I was in over my head. Indeed, the snares of death encompassed me, but in my distress, I called upon the LORD my God. I cried for help, and from His temple He heard my voice and my cry to Him reached His ears. He sent from on high. He took me. He drew me out of many waters. He rescued me from my strong enemy and from those who hated me for they were too mighty for me. They confronted me in the day of my calamity, but the LORD was my support! (Psalm 18:5-6, 16-18).

I felt quite panicked, as I gathered up a few diapers, while wondering how I was going to transport my two children; one barely walked, and the other did not walk at all. I was contemplating carrying them in a laundry basket when something alarming occurred. My 9-month-old son became pale and limp while drinking a freshly made bottle. Had his formula been poisoned like our food had been so many times before? I ran to a neighboring apartment to ask them to call 911. Shortly thereafter, we were on our way to the hospital. I was in constant prayer within. He seemed to be perking up a little bit, and I watched in the hospital room as a migrating rash would disappear and reappear in another area of his tiny body until, finally, it subsided. For this, I was thankful and rejoicing.

After much thankfulness in my heart to God for healing my boy and for getting us out of our apartment successfully (had this hospital detour not taken place, we almost certainly would have been intercepted), my thoughts now turned to, what do I do now, LORD? Calling the authorities was out of the question as this man's connections and the corruption in the area made him untouchable. I could never go back home, and there was not one single person on this earth I could call, not one. But I was not alone. My God was with me.

We left the hospital at twilight, and I carried them in car seats. They were so heavy; I would carry them ten steps and need to put them down for several seconds. Although I could not see how God was going to work this situation out, I knew in my heart that I needed to trust Him and continue to put one foot in front of the other, literally. We got to the top of a steep hill and around the corner when all of a sudden, God moved. Incredibly, a kind woman offered me her stroller sensing that we were in distress. I thanked God for her and for this stroller, and I began to walk in tune to the LORD's guidance and direction.

There is a verse in Deuteronomy that speaks volumes to my heart. It is found in Ch. 32:10-12, and it goes like this: He found him (her) in a desert land and in the howling waste of wilderness. He encircled him (her). He cared for him (her). He kept him (her) as the apple of His eye. Like an eagle that stirs up its nest, that flutters over its young, spreading out its wings, catching them, bearing them on its pinions, the LORD alone guided him (her). No foreign god was with him (her). The LORD alone guided me; no foreign god was with me. Praise the LORD.

I began to walk, and then I walked some more. The evening became night, the night became day, and the day became night again. It was hot, it was hard, and it was exhausting, but it was a beautiful time spent with my God. I spent many amazing hours in worship of and in fellowship with the LORD. It felt as if nothing stood between us, and I was grateful for the intimacy.

His tender, compassionate grace was poured over us in abundance, and He brought inconceivable peace to all three of us in the midst of a difficult situation. I cannot adequately describe the overall sense of peace that surpassed human understanding, but it was undeniable (not just within me but noticeably in and around my children as well). There were parts of this journey that were extremely difficult; tears were shed and fears came upon me, but I knew that God was right there with me every step of the way. He was encouraging me, strengthening me, and helping us to avoid the dangers we faced. It was raw vulnerability, a total state of helplessness, and He supplied the grace and strength necessary. He upheld me with His righteous right hand as we walked many miles.

The indescribable intimacy we shared on this walk was the beginning of a beautiful relationship with my Savior, my greatest treasure of all. As we journeyed the unknown, I was given the ability to sing His praises. This calmed my fears and increased my gratitude for what He had done. If He did not do even one more thing for us and if He would decree indefinite suffering for the rest of my life, I was content in my salvation. I was completely content and totally at peace. The sense I had of His presence was overwhelming and breathtaking. All I had was Christ, and He was more than enough.

As I walked, I could sense the darkness, and I could sense the evil surrounding me, but it seemed as if my children and I were walking within a bubble of light. I felt completely protected, and this I called to mind: Even though I walk through the valley of the shadow of death, I will fear no evil for you are with me. A children's song also kept coming to mind; only a boy named David, only a little sling, only a boy named David, but he could pray and sing. Yes, and just like David, I too could pray and sing, and that is exactly what I did. Oh, the wonderful, unfathomable peace which surpasses all understanding. I had no idea, not so much as a thought, about what to do next, but

I knew I completely trusted Him for all of it. If I could trust Him for eternal salvation, I could trust Him for the rest, come what may. I did not know it at the time, but David speaks of this very thing in II Samuel 22 and Psalm 18; God has given me the shield of His salvation. As my understanding deepened regarding the gift of my salvation, it really did become a shield off which the fears and the circumstances just sort of bounced. Praise the LORD!

At roughly hour thirty-three of this journey, around 3 a.m., I was experiencing a whole new level of exhaustion. I had a few hundred dollars to my name at that point and I said, "LORD, you know how tired I am. May we please go to a hotel for a few hours, so I can rest, and will you please protect us?" I felt a peaceful yes. What a relief to be able to lie down, to be able to let the children spread out upon a bed, to get a break from the heat, and to be able to take a shower.

Checkout was 11 a.m., but I decided we should not stay past 7 a.m. I thought to myself, I can sleep from 3 to 6 a.m. Huh. I said to the LORD, "I do not know what you could possibly do, but I know you can do anything; I have not slept in two days, and I need to be restored. Please help. Thank you, Father. Good night." I shut my eyes, and for the next three hours, I woke up every ten to fifteen minutes. Yet, every time I woke up, it felt like I had been sleeping for many hours. It was as if my Father had stopped time itself for me. I felt a warm, peaceful feeling in my heart, and with a smile on my face, I would fall back asleep. Three hours later, I woke up feeling totally refreshed, and He was now putting the next step in my mind.

We left the hotel at 7 a.m. and headed to a place of business where I was almost certain I could make some phone calls. They agreed and also provided a list of possible shelters, which I did not know existed.

Two hours and thirty calls later, I was again told, "No, we do not have space available." This was extremely discouraging. However, she then offered me the number to a shelter that was not on my list. I was feeling disappointed, but I continued to trust and pray, asking God to please open a door for me. I dialed the number and an incredibly kind and compassionate voice was on the other end. They were also at capacity, but after hearing a little bit of my story, she said, "If you can get here today, we will make room for you." Wow. It certainly felt like a breakthrough moment; the LORD had parted the mighty waters after helping us make our escape from "Egypt," and it certainly would not be the last time He made a way when there seemed to be no way.

We were put up on an air mattress in a classroom initially and later transferred to a regular room. Praise the LORD! Just like that, God provided shelter, food, and free clothes from a thrift store. Also, in exchange for chores, I could earn points at the shelter for diapers, wipes, and formula. In an instant, God had spoken all of our needs into existence. Incredible! It blew me away, and He has been blowing my mind ever since. And my God shall supply every need of yours according to His riches in glory in Christ Jesus (Philippians 4:19). This was a six-week shelter, and during that time I called many out-of-state shelters to begin our life in a new location. I prayed, "LORD, please close every door that does not belong to me and open only the one that does. I will go wherever you want me to go so long as you are with me."

Being around other women who were broken and abused was an opportunity to share the hope I had found in Christ alone – A hope I wanted everyone to know and experience. I am a total introvert, so it was not as if I was striking up conversation, but as God did the striking, I found myself, indeed, speaking of my Savior's loving-kindness toward me. Out of the abundance of the heart, the mouth speaks.

The LORD opened another door for us, and at the five-week mark we boarded a bus, embarking upon a twenty-nine-hour journey to an unknown land. My daughter had just turned 2 years old and my son was now 10 months old. This could make for a difficult time on a long bus ride, but God kindly poured out His grace, and it was, indeed, more than sufficient. Again, the peace radiated from within as my children were calm, able to sleep, and even found the ride to be fun and enjoyable.

We arrived at the safehouse, a beautiful home, where we would stay for the next two weeks. This particular shelter made decisions based on financial gain. The more people they put through, the more funding they received. Therefore, the majority of the residents were given the boot at the two-week mark. There would begin here a testing of my responses in the face of difficult situations with difficult people, and God would begin the maturing process of my faith. Would I respond like Amy or like Jesus?

Additionally, He began strongly directing me to read His Word. There was only one problem with this. After He began to show me just how deceived I had been and just how many lies we are fed daily throughout the course of our lives, I said in my alarm all mankind are liars (Psalm 116:10). My train of thought was that it might, in fact, be God's Word, but surely it had been corrupted and tainted by human injection. However, He would not let up, so I asked the staff if they had a Bible, and I got a strange look and a big no. You can imagine my surprise when, later that day, a Bible was placed into my hands by the very same staff member. God's purposes simply cannot be thwarted. Praise the LORD.

Once I got my hands on it, the prayer was this – "LORD, if there is so much as a hint of a lie in this thing, I expect you to tell me; do not let me be deceived." He did me one better and something very interesting began to take place. During the day, He would bring a particular scripture to mind. Then, later that night, I would read in His Word the very same scripture. This did not happen only once or twice. This continued to happen most days of the week on a consistent basis, and it still happens to me today. And now I have told you before it takes place, so that when it does take place you may believe (John 14:29). In addition, as I read through it, He was giving me relevant circumstances in which I had the opportunity to put His Word into action.

One evening, as a woman told me about the intense stomach pain she was experiencing as the result of a botched surgery, God gave me a sincere compassion for her. I felt an overwhelming desire to pray for her. He then also prompted me to ask a question. As she was talking to me, I was talking to God, and I asked Him internally, "Should I pray for her now or later?" I thought, later. That did not seem right to me, so I asked Him again. "Should I pray for her now or later?" I thought, later, so I let it go.

After we went our separate ways, I went up to my room and began to read His Word. I read the following: But when you pray, go into your room and shut the door and pray to your Father who is in secret, and your Father who sees in secret will reward you (Matthew 6:6). The lightbulb went on. I then prayed for her concerning three specific things, which included the request that she would be able to sleep without waking up and without pain. When I saw her the next morning, I asked how she was feeling and how she slept. She proceeded to tell me she was shocked because for the first time in months she had slept all the way through the night without one episode of pain. She also mentioned two other things which shocked her. These were the very things for which I had petitioned God on her behalf. We praised and glorified God together, and the thought flashed back in my mind – You are a prayer warrior, my dear daughter.

At the end of two weeks, I had no idea where we would go. The places I called were at capacity, and I did not know what to do next. Someone told me of a shelter sixty miles north of us, so I called them, but they denied having space available. I hoped we would look pitiful enough to be taken in if we showed up on the doorstep. We set out, and I remember feeling completely at peace, trusting the LORD to come through for us in some way.

By the grace of God, we found the place (I am still not using a phone at this point). To my dismay, their pity did not provide us a room. It was dark now, and I thought to myself, well, I guess we will be doing some more walking tonight. However, they told me of an overnight shelter that I could try, located one and a half miles away. We set out again, and I sang and worshiped all the way there. They took us in for the night, and the next day the staff referred me to a place that could take us in for sixty days. Wow. That was such a long time compared to the experience so far. It was a house, and there was even a swing set for the children.

As the LORD continued to speak to me daily through His Word in such a personal and powerful way, I began to obtain Bibles and place them in the hands of others with a note written inside, specific to the individual. I was beginning to understand the importance of God's Word. By the grace of God, this is a ministry I have continued to practice through the years as I am led to do so by the LORD.

It was at this point that my faith in God, the Son (Jesus Christ), would be tried. Even though I knew my salvation rested on the work of Christ on the cross and His resurrection and even though I spent that initial night of total surrender singing "Turn Your Eyes Upon Jesus" by Helen Lemmel, somehow, the enemy was using the skewed philosophies of others to try to sow seeds of doubt. Thanks be to God, I was committed to His Word at this point, and all those fiery doubts would be quickly debunked and extinguished. Hopefully, I was able to sow my own seeds of the truth about Jesus Christ into their lives. See to it that no one takes you captive by philosophy and empty deceit, according to human tradition, according to the elemental spirits of the world and not according to Christ (Colossians 2:8).

I attempted to find work, for which I was repeatedly turned down. I even tried to volunteer, for which I was turned away. I said, "God, I do not understand. Why do I keep hitting these dead ends?" In my spirit, loud and clear, I heard, am I not taking good enough care of you? I was speechless, and my heart melted. I was overwhelmed by the wonderful care of My Provider.

During our stay here, the LORD revealed our next destination. This happened to be several states away. My efforts centered on figuring out how I was going to get there. These efforts would prove futile because the timing was off. If God calls you to do something, He will enable you to do it in His time. This is a truth I did not realize or understand just yet. I figured since He had revealed this to me, I was now responsible to make it happen, but that is just not the case at all. We see that very thing take place, for instance, in the story of Abraham and Sarah. God revealed to them that they would have a son, and twenty-four years later, they did, but first they would take matters into their own hands. There is an important lesson here, and it is this: Attempting to bring God's promises to fruition in our own strength and timing is futile and never ends well. We must learn to patiently wait upon the LORD. More on this later.

I also learned here to guard my heart against grumbling. The food was unquestionably bland, and I found myself internally complaining. Oh, if I only had onions and garlic, I could make this stuff taste better. I reminisced in my mind about the food stamps I used to have to get anything I wanted at the store, but now I was no longer on food stamps because I was trying to keep a low profile. Later that night, I *happened to be* in Numbers 11, and I read this: The people of Israel wept again and said, oh that we had meat to eat! We remember the fish we ate in Egypt that cost us nothing, the cucumbers, the melons, the leeks, the onions, and the garlic. My jaw literally dropped. I was immediately convicted to my core, and I quickly repented. I thought, how dare I? Look around at all of these blessings and consider the fact that you have any food at all. How about the fact that your life is not being threatened? Or how about the fact that the LORD has delivered you from a great oppression and has revealed His presence to you? And I have the nerve to complain in my heart about onions and garlic? Sigh . . .

For those who may not know how that story ends – The anger of the LORD blazed hotly and because they rejected the LORD who was among them and wept before Him saying why did we come out of Egypt. He sent loads and loads of quail, and while the meat was still between their teeth, He struck them with a very great plague. I felt sorrowful, and I threw myself on the mercy of the LORD. He, of course, granted forgiveness, and I prayed, "LORD, please keep me grateful and content in all situations. Do not let my heart grumble against you. I am so sorry." The funny thing was that later that week He would lead me to a food bank where I would receive . . . onions and garlic. He could have provided this right off the bat, but then I would have missed out on an important lesson. The LORD is intentional in His ways with us, if only we have ears to hear and eyes to see.

When my sixty days were over, we would spend two more nights in the overnight shelter where we would make another connection and be accepted into another house where we spent the next three weeks. This is where I finished reading the Bible for the first time, which took around four months. (I highly recommend reading the entire Bible in a short span of time – You retain more of what you read, and it fits together more fluidly). My eyes had been opened to so many things I did not know were in there. He says, call to me, and I will answer you, and I will tell you great and hidden things you have not known (Jeremiah 33:3). My heart stands in awe of His Word, and I rejoice at His Word like one who has found great spoil; I just love it. If you get nothing else from this book, I hope you get this – Learn to love the Word of God! It is breathtaking and full of awesome wonder.

From here, we would go to another house for four weeks. If you think all the moving was difficult, it was, but I am certain that it was the perfect will of God as He did all the leading. Thankfully, God's grace was more than sufficient, and our time at these places was not wasted. There were many opportunities to share God's love with women and children who were hurting, and it truly blessed me; I pray it did them as well.

From there, we were accepted into a three-month program. Praise the LORD! Three whole months! It gets even better, however, because that three months turned into six months. It was a much welcome break from the frequent moving. It was here that I would read the Bible a second time and part of a third time. I also began to write in a journal the verses that stuck out to me each day. I spent a lot of time in God's Word; I could not get enough of it.

Living with other women can be interesting, and I was given many opportunities to put what I was reading into practice. Sometimes I did this well and other times not so well, but I learned to repent quickly and take every negative or hateful thought captive to obey Christ. I would often say, "Father, forgive me. Please help me to think less like me and more like you."

Hebrews 10:25 stuck out to me at this time, which says, do not neglect meeting together as is the habit of some. I loved my new relationship with my Savior, and I loved His Word, but I thought church was full of hypocrites; I did not want to be a part of that. However, I felt like God was telling me to go, so I went to the one to which He led me. It is true that many churches have gone off course, so please be careful with whom you align yourself. Pray that God would lead you to where He wants you. He will. It was a short-lived obedience as COVID would shut it down, but I did enjoy the time I spent there. It was a nice change of pace to be around others who had a love for Jesus Christ, unlike the many lost with whom I had been living. It was certainly encouraging.

After a couple of months, the church opened back up, and we began outside services. In addition, the LORD put it in their hearts to provide the next set of bus tickets for me and my children to get to our next destination several states away. In His time, He brought forth the arrangements and smoothly worked out all the details because He is powerful and completely sovereign (in control). I had learned an invaluable lesson. If God reveals your course (His will) to you while He is driving, do not attempt to take the steering wheel as if you must now figure out how to get there. Allow Him to stay in the driver's seat and sit back and enjoy the ride.

Everyone I knew at the time felt I was somewhat crazy to leave for another state without a plan. However, I was certain God told me to go, and I knew He had a plan. I knew the city and the state to which He called me but not anything beyond that. I knew I was not supposed to try to make arrangements ahead of time; rather, I was just supposed to go. My response to the people who questioned my sanity was this: I may not have a plan, but I am sure my God does. I was sincerely confident in Him. I was consistently asking the LORD to increase my faith, and I was drawn to the storm story in the gospels. As fears tried to creep into my mind about this journey I was about to embark upon, I spent that much more time in His Word, and the God of endurance and encouragement assured me through so many wonderful scriptures. He reminded me that my times are in His hand, and He told me to be strong and courageous and not to be afraid for He would go with me wherever I go.

I did not want to be a disciple of little faith freaked out by the storm while knowing Jesus is in the boat with me, so I prayed for faith, and faith He supplied. He used many verses to ease my uneasiness. Isaiah 43:1-3, for example, became quite precious to me. But now thus says the LORD, He who created you . . . He who formed you . . . Fear not, for I have redeemed you; I have called you by name, you are mine. When you pass through the waters, I will be with you; and through the rivers, they shall not overwhelm you; when you walk through the fire you shall not be burned, and the flame shall not consume you. For I am the LORD your God, the Holy One of Israel, your Savior.

We embarked upon a thirty-hour adventure, and again His grace was marvelously sufficient. My active toddlers, ages 1 and 2 years old at the time, were calm and peaceful for the duration of this bus ride, which was quite astounding. There was a peace on this journey inside and out that could not be explained beyond the grace of God beautifully working down to the smallest detail. His glorious presence was palpable, and I was overwhelmed by His lovingkindness.

For the last two hours of the trip, the bus cleared out, and only my children and I remained. Then, they fell asleep. This was unusual because it was 10 a.m. God knew this is exactly what I needed, however, because I was about to engage in some serious warfare.

I was feeling secure when, suddenly, it was as if an army surrounded me, and the arrows of fire came flying at me one after another on every side. I found myself in the midst of an intense spiritual battle. A sudden fear would arise, which was extinguished by a response of faith, my shield. This was followed by another attack and another and another. Did God really tell you to come here? Have you lost your mind? What if this? What if that? What were you thinking? I pored over the scriptures in my Bible, sang songs of praise, and prayed and worshiped through raging tears. While I was feeling completely overwhelmed by various fears, I was fighting and speaking truth into the lies. I knew He had gone before me to prepare a resting place for us, and I knew He was totally on my side. The LORD is on my side; I will not fear. What can man do to me? (Psalm 118:6). Interestingly, earlier that morning, I had come across Ephesians 6 in my reading: Finally, be strong in the LORD and in the strength of His might for we do not wrestle against flesh and blood. Put on the full armor of God. In all circumstances, take up the shield of faith and the sword of the Spirit, praying at all times in the Spirit. Now, here I was a couple of hours later, by the grace of God, putting it all into practice. I knew I could trust Him and whatever plans He had for us, but I was feeling something emotionally that did not line up. It was war. It was all-out war. The victory belongs to the LORD!

We were five minutes away when the tears began to dry up, and there was a ceasefire. It was as if Jesus just stood up and said, Peace! Be still! I felt a great calm, for which I was so thankful. He will still the storm to a whisper, and the waves of the sea will be hushed (Psalm 107:29) in His time. There is no telling what that bus driver must have been thinking as he caught glimpses of me in his rearview mirror.

At any rate, we arrived. I felt calm but still totally clueless. I did have an address given to me the day we left for this adventure, but there was no telling what would come of that. I asked someone if they were familiar with where that street was located. It was only a few blocks away. We walked up there; it was an office. We looked a little rough from the journey, so the kind woman asked me with a concerned look on her face, "Can I help you?" I said, "Well, I hope so."

I could not believe what would happen next. After a short five-minute phone call, I was informed, "Yes, we will accept you, but because you have come from another state, we must first put you up in a hotel due to COVID restrictions. A taxi will be by to pick you up shortly." Wow. An hour later we were settled into a room and able to take a shower. They brought us three meals per day, and we were less than a mile from a gorgeous and breathtaking body of water. I love being in God's presence in God's creation, and I love being around water, so this was a wonderful gift. It had a beautiful shoreline of rocks, trees, and flowers, and all I could think was, wow! Oh, you of little faith. Not only did He seek out a resting place for you, but he provided you with a beautiful vacation!

Here is an excerpt from my journal on day seven of our ten-day hotel stay: I am meditating on all the things I am thankful for and this beautiful vacation you have given us. You told me to come here to an unknown land and people with no plan, assuring me all along that you had a plan, so I put all my trust in you, and we have been absolutely blessed. It is so beautiful here, and you are right here with us. I am so grateful for your presence, Father. I love you. Thank you.

On day ten, we moved into the shelter one mile up the road. I met a prostitute who was at a desperate point in her life, and God gave me an opportunity to share with her the hope and the peace I had found in a relationship with Jesus Christ. For a few days, the LORD had been urging me to talk with her, but there never seemed to be a good time. Finally, I prayed about it. "LORD, if you want me to talk with her, then please, I need you to open a door." He sure did. she said something which prompted a conversation that opened a door for a natural response of encouragement through my own experience, which was similar to hers. She was in over her head, and there was only one solution – Jesus Christ. I gave her a Bible later that evening and encouraged her to submit to Christ. She left the next morning and never returned. I pray she found The Way. It is so important that we pray like the apostle Paul did and ask God to open a door for the gospel.

This was only a thirty-day shelter, but by week three, I had been accepted into another, and there was a possibility of being approved for their two-year transitional program. Without an income, however, I was turned down. This was a huge disappointment, but the manager of the house handed me a phone number on a sticky note which lifted me up. Printed on the bottom of the stationery was this – Behold, I am with you always to the end of the age. Immediately, I felt His warm, reassuring presence.

I then sat outside with my nose in His Word because that is where I am comforted, and I came upon Hebrews 6:18-19. We who have fled for refuge have strong encouragement to hold fast to the hope set before us. We have this as a sure and steadfast anchor of the soul, a hope that enters into the inner place behind the curtain. As I read those words, *enters into the inner place behind the curtain*, I was filled with peace and total awe. It was a beautifully intimate moment, and I would go on to say this in my journal: Thank you for your peace in my life, which is so full of uncertainty. Of this I am certain – You will be with me always, and you are all I need.

I was now beginning to see a pattern in my life. I said, "LORD, when I surrendered my life and agreed to follow you anywhere, I thought there would be a final destination where we might stay put. But if it is your will that I continue to be a mobile witness, then I know you will give me the strength and the grace to do your will." He then reminded me that while foxes have holes and birds of the air have nests, the Son of Man (Jesus) had nowhere to lay His head. Why shouldn't I be a wandering spokesperson for the LORD? My final destination is Heaven, for here we have no lasting city but we seek the city that is to come.

After a short phone interview, I was accepted into a shelter four hours away. That night I was reading in Numbers 9. At the command of the LORD, the people of Israel set out, and at the command of the LORD, they camped. As long as the cloud rested over the tabernacle, they remained . . . sometimes the cloud was a few days and sometimes the cloud remained from evening to morning . . . whether it was two days or a month or a longer time, the people of Israel remained, but when it lifted, they set out. I love God's Word.

A nice couple from church would agree to help me get there. During the car ride, they asked questions that would really get me talking. It was all good conversation about God, but there was just one problem. Never once did I whisper a prayer to Him throughout all four hours. By the time we got to the shelter, all I could think of was the scripture that says, a fool is known by his (or her) many words. I felt sick, and I felt sick of myself. I would later understand that it was pride. My heart had lifted itself up after all the LORD had been showing me and teaching me. Though I was talking all about God on that ride, I was not talking with God. How frightening that we can be so full of pride and have no idea. We must continually seek humility through prayer. We have no good apart from Him. None.

This failure to pray continued into my intake meeting, and I presumptuously entered a conversation without asking God's guidance or direction. I sensed, yet disregarded, that the woman sitting before me was strangely full of darkness, yet I did not acknowledge

Him at all. Just a few days later, she became a serious threat to our safety.

The thing about this location is that we were kind of in the middle of nowhere. There were cornfields in every direction for miles, and the thought of leaving on foot again with no idea where we were going was almost unbearable. Still, I got a strong sense that we needed to get away from there asap.

As we walked around the town one day, there were bees flying around us relentlessly. This is interesting, and you will see why in a moment. When we got back, I looked to the Word of God for clarity and direction. I do not usually do this, but feeling desperate and not knowing where to turn, I "randomly" opened my Bible. Through tears, I read what was on the page in front of me.

O God, insolent men have risen against me . . . turn to me and be gracious to me. Give strength to your servant (Psalm 86). The next "random" opening would take me to Psalm 118. Out of my distress, I called on the LORD. The LORD answered me and set me free. The LORD is on my side. I will not fear . . . The LORD is on my side as my helper . . . It is better to take refuge in the LORD than to trust in man . . . *They surrounded me like bees* (italics added). I was pushed hard so that I was falling, but the LORD helped me. The LORD is my strength and my song . . . O LORD, we pray give us success.

Then I read, because He is at my right hand, I shall not be shaken (Psalm 16:8). I was not just reading through tears but praying these words to Him, and He was simultaneously comforting me and impressing upon me that we would leave everything and follow Him somewhere else. As I inquired if I was hearing Him correctly, I came upon Joshua 1:16, which states, all that you have commanded us, we will do, and wherever you send us, we will go. Then in verse 9, I read, be strong and courageous. Do not be afraid or dismayed, for the LORD your God is with you wherever you go. My next step was completely clear, and His perfect peace flooded my being.

I wrote this in my journal: You are in charge of my story. It is not up to me to make it happen – I know I trust you, but I want to trust you more. I want to be unshakable in your Name. My weaknesses overwhelm me, but your grace is sufficient. The waters feel deep, but you are with us always. You will never leave us nor forsake us.

Jesus did not say that following Him would be easy. It may seem safer to keep our usual routines rather than take a risk by acting in obedient faith, but if we faithfully persevere, the reward is great. I came across Psalm 46 as I read my Bible into the late-night hours. God is our refuge and strength, an ever-present (well-proved) help in trouble. Therefore, we will not fear though the earth gives way and the mountains fall into the sea . . . God is in the midst of her. She shall not be moved. God will help her when morning dawns. I found this a comfort knowing we would be setting out at dawn, and I glorified God.

When dawn came, we set out. My children are acclimated to much walking, so this was not out of the norm for them. We just did what we always do, pray and sing. I had no idea where to go. I did not even know where we were on a map. I just asked God for direction, and we went that way. We sang, "God Will Make A Way" by Don Moen. "O, God will make a way when there seems to be no way. He works in ways we cannot see. He will make a way for me. He will be my guide, hold me closely to His side. With love and strength for each new day, He will make a way. By a roadway in the wilderness, you lead me. Everywhere I look, you're all I see. Heaven and earth will fade, but His Word will still remain, and He will do something new today."

This was very much a roadway in the wilderness, a two-lane highway with barely a shoulder to walk on and corn as far as the eye could see. It was daunting. I asked God to send someone to us. We walked maybe a mile on the gravelly terrain, which completely tore up the little wheels on the stroller, when suddenly a kind woman pulled over and offered us a ride. She took us an hour away to a bus station where God would make another connection for me. The woman behind the counter knew exactly who I needed to call.

That afternoon, we were headed to a hotel that had been made into a shelter. We would have our own little apartment, and it was a beautiful and peaceful area. There were lots of trees, and the leaves were beginning to change color. The woman who did my intake paperwork was so caring, and we were immediately hooked up with everything we needed and so much more. We also found a double stroller with bicycle tires in decent condition, which was being given away.

An excerpt from my journal says this: You truly do amaze me every day. The few hours of sleep I got felt like eight, and you sustained me in your strength all throughout the day. You faithfully led me by a roadway in the wilderness of corn and sent help rapidly. You faithfully guided every step, and now here we are, just like you said. Thank you for being a faithful, loving, and trustworthy God. I need you always. I want you to lead me and be near me always. One of the verses I read tonight is from Hebrews 4:12; the Word of God is alive and active. Yeah, it is! Crazy how much so! I am in awe of you, LORD, total awe!

I was blown away by the stuff. We were provided with food, clothes, toiletries, children's books and toys, and many other things along with our own space and our own bathroom. I was feeling ecstatic for days. I was elated, so thankful, and completely grateful. There was a problem, however. Something was not right. I could feel it in my spirit. Something was not sitting quite right regarding the level of happiness I felt over these material things.

We were on a walk to one of the many beautiful and unusual parks in the area when I had the thought, it almost feels wrong to be so excited about the stuff, even with the gratitude aimed wholly at God. Do not love the world or the things in the world . . . For all that is in the world, the desires of the flesh and the desires of the eyes, and the pride of life (possessions) is not from the Father but is from the world, and the world is passing away with all its desires (I John 2:15-17).

That night, I threw myself on His mercy and repented for the joy I was experiencing because of possessions. He, of course, compassionately forgave me. However, He then impressed upon me that I would be leaving in the morning and that I would not be taking anything with me – Nothing. I certainly did not want to leave, but it was clear to me that I was to trust and obey. I wrote a note to myself in my journal that night – Focus on God's power, not on the storm.

Through many wonders, we ended up at another shelter. This one, however, felt extremely institutional. There was nothing warm or welcoming about it, but it was a roof over our heads, and I was grateful for it. The next ten days were a time of humbling. Up to this point, we had been spoiled with food, toiletries, and clothes that were always perfect in every way. This was not that way at all, which was totally intentional on His part and necessary. Where was my joy found? Where was my security? Was it in Christ alone or was it in Christ plus _____ (fill in the blank)? The LORD told me to stand strong. He forewarned me through His Word that this would be a difficult time but that I would not have to stay here for long.

I read the first five books of the Bible that week. I prayed, I fasted, and I sought the LORD with all my heart. Through Hebrews 12:5-6, 11, He said, "My child, do not regard lightly my discipline or be weary when reproved by me, for I discipline those whom I love. For the moment, all discipline seems painful rather than pleasant but later it yields the peaceful fruit of righteousness to those who have been trained by it." He also showed me Job 5:17-18: "Behold, blessed is the one God reproves. Therefore, despise not the discipline of the Almighty, for He wounds, but He binds up. He shatters, but His hands heal." He also said to me, through Deuteronomy 5:29, "Oh, that you had such a heart as this always, to fear me and keep all my commandments."

A shocking thing would occur during my stay here. For twenty-three years, I had been a smoker. When I surrendered my life whole-heartedly one year prior, I did not have a sudden conviction to im-mediately quit smoking; nevertheless, I sensed from Him that there would come a point when He would ask me to do so. The thought was incomprehensible. I was completely yoked to this stronghold at a pack a day. Every time I tried to quit, I could not. I was sure I would smoke until the day I died. God had other plans. Wouldn't you know it, this was the week He would impress upon me, ok, now I want you to quit.

Nadab and Abihu were sons of Aaron, who were a part of the priesthood in the Old Testament. The LORD struck them dead when they offered unauthorized (strange) fire before the LORD. Every time I lit up a cigarette, I repeatedly heard in my spirit, "Unauthorized fire . . . unauthorized fire." I thought, surely not, LORD, not now; I am under significant stress. That must just be in my mind because I have been reading the first five books of the Old Testament. Surely, you do not mean . . . Oh yes. He sure did mean it. I would later learn obedience because I love Him, but for right now, honestly, I was concerned about repercussions for not doing what He clearly told me He wanted me to do – Quit. So, I did just that. Then, I was feeling undoubtedly low. This thing was a part of me, it seemed, and therein lies the problem.

After a week in this institutional place of humbling, He lifted my head, and I read, I will again take delight in prospering you . . . when you obey the voice of the LORD your God to keep His commandments and His statutes written in this book of the Law when you turn to the LORD your God with all your heart and with all your soul. For this commandment that I command you today is not too hard for you, neither is it far off, but the Word is very near you. It is in your mouth and in your heart, so that you can do it. See, I have set before you today life and good, death and evil (Deuteronomy 30). Then, I felt the nudge. It was time to go. We left, and I was thankful to have learned what I had. In addition, my joy in Christ alone had been rekindled, which felt incredible.

We set out, and the LORD was my guide in a totally unknown place again (still no phone), and by His great power, He would lead us straight into a bus stop a couple of miles away. I was not sure where it would take us, but we would soon find out. Through a miracle of God, we were accepted into a shelter. I was so thankful, and you had better believe I was praying, "LORD, please let us stay here for a time." He did.

The humbling process continued, and He was enabling me to be obedient out of reverence and gratitude, not so much for fear of repercussion. He also began to show me, and it began to sink in, that we should not conform to this world. So many of us are conforming to the world around us. We are supposed to live as a people holy (set apart) to the LORD. We should look and act and speak differently from everyone else. You shall be holy to me for I, the LORD, am holy and have separated you from the peoples that you should be mine (Leviticus 20:26).

This was a house full of women, so there was a chance for ministry once more. There were difficulties, and in more than one instance, I was hated without a cause, but in this I rejoiced. Jesus said, "Blessed are you when others revile you and persecute you and utter all kinds of evil against you falsely on my account. Rejoice and be glad, for your reward is great in heaven." He also said, "If the world hates you, know that it has hated me before it hated you," and I took great comfort in these words.

I grappled with how to be salt and light and how to love my enemies with the love of Jesus Christ, but by the grace of God, I was able to do this very thing. He often brought Romans 12:14 to mind. Bless those who persecute you; bless, and do not curse them! The most loving thing I can do for my enemies is pray for them, asking God to grant them repentance leading to a knowledge of the truth. It is truly interesting, however, to watch Jesus cause your enemies to be at peace with you (Proverbs 16:7).

God wants us to go to Him first about everything we deal with, and this includes difficulty with others. In a communal living setting, issues are bound to arise; some are justified and some are petty. Either way, issues are inevitable. I learned how to trust God with all of it. Instead of seeking another human to talk with about what I was enduring, I chose to talk with my God about it, who already knew fully what I was experiencing. The super unexpected thing I came across time and time again was that he would often step in and do something about it. I can even think of three different occasions in three different shelters where someone was particularly hateful and evil. After taking my concerns to God alone, said people were kicked out. He completely removed the problem. That is not to say He will always remove our problems. Of course, He does not. Often, there is something to be learned as we deal with it, but it never ceased to blow my mind just how involved He is.

We are so inclined in our flesh to run to other humans amidst turmoil. Though I used to be extremely guilty of doing this, I have learned the value of taking my issues to God alone. That is not to say that we do not seek godly counsel when appropriate; however, go to Him first! It is a level of trust not often seen in today's age, but you will not be disappointed. It will only serve to deepen and strengthen your relationship with Him.

I spent many hours each day in the Word, and I began writing verses that stood out on index cards. This took me seven months to complete, but today I have four thick stacks of cards full of scriptures from every book of the Bible. These have continued to bless me in amazing ways as the LORD has orchestrated those scriptures to speak into my present circumstances daily.

As I began to wake up one morning, I heard a city and a state within my inner being. I inquired, "Do you want me to go there?" Later that day, I saw that very license plate right outside my window, which was unusual because this state happened to be several states away. I kept the matter in mind.

I was offered a spot in a two-year transitional program, but every time I asked the LORD if I should accept this offer, it seemed as if He said no. The shelter where I was staying was a three-month stay, and I had totally dumbfounded the staff in turning this down. I was even a little thrown off myself because that sounded like a good idea to me. I asked the LORD many times over a two-month period if I should accept this offer, and every time, He seemed to be saying no.

I was now at the end of my stay in this home, and I had made sixteen phone calls to other shelters, all of which turned me down. I had no clear direction to go to that new state just yet, so I was not going to push for that outside of God's timing, but I was unsure of what to do next. There did remain one possible option with another shelter in the area. A staff member took me there, and after much prayer, I would wait in line to speak to the woman in charge.

Initially, she said, "I do not think I can help you." As totally unexpected tears came to my eyes, I felt confident that God would open a door somewhere, and I said, "That's okay. Thank you for your time. God must have another plan." In that very instant, I felt the Holy Spirit move, and she got a twinkle in her eye. She said, "Okay, I have a little room I can put you in, and also I want to give you $800 to get you started." Just like that, we were given $800 and a key to our own apartment, complete with laundry and play area out back. This "little" room was the largest we had been in to date, and it had a stove, a fridge, our own bathroom, and a landline telephone. I was so thankful, but certainly with the prayer that I would keep the provision from God of physical things in perspective. We simply cannot serve two masters. Where our treasure is, there our heart will be also. God himself deserves to be our one and only treasure. *It is imperative that we desire the presence of the LORD over and above His presents.*

Commit your way to the LORD. Trust in Him, and He will act! (Psalm 37:5). Do you trust God Almighty with all of your heart? That is what He is after . . . your heart. Eve was led astray when she stopped believing that God had her best interest at heart. Of course, God loved her perfectly and only wanted the best for her, but her unbelief led to disobedience. Therefore, sin and the curse came upon mankind, and the cycle has continued for thousands of years. Glory to God, He demolished the curse of sin leading to death through the precious blood of His one and only Son, Jesus Christ.

How many of us are being led astray when something hard or painful takes place? Instead of leaning that much closer into our relationship with the LORD, pouring out our hearts before Him, the God of all comfort, we turn to our idols and turn away from Him. We may even start to think He must have abandoned us, does not really love us, or does not want what is best for us. These are all lies from the enemy. Think back to the garden. Did God really say _____ (fill in the blank)? If you are not immersed daily in the Word of God, continuously pumping His truth into your veins, the deceitfulness of sin will diminish the truth about God in your heart, leading to unbelief and a lack of trust. If we do not stay firmly rooted in the Word of God, we will even start to question His goodness, His faithfulness, and His perfect will, especially in the face of affliction.

We must stay grounded and totally anchored to the Word of God, standing firm on His promises. In addition, we must take up the shield of faith, with which we can extinguish ALL the flaming arrows of the evil one. If you are a child of God, you will be attacked. It is unavoidable. The weapons you use to combat make all the difference. Do you lack faith? Ask for it. God will provide. Do you lack knowledge of the scriptures? Read it, a lot. Do not take it for granted. We are heading into a different age. Get to know God's Word now and make the best use of your time because the days are evil.

Many of us go to great lengths throughout the course of our lives attempting to stay as comfortable as possible. We seek to avoid or alleviate any and all pain and suffering at any cost. We let fear and anxiety keep us paralyzed when we should be moving forward, ever pressing harder into our relationship with the LORD, who sees us through it all. This attempt to avoid suffering causes us great harm and spiritual decline because it is in the fire we are refined; it is in the storm our faith is increased; it is in our weakness His power is made perfect; and it is in the struggle that our spiritual self matures. We must never lose sight of this, no, not ever.

There is a place where the curse is gone, and sin is no more. There is no more crying, no more pain, and no more sorrow. It is called Heaven. Perfection is God's design and has been His plan since the beginning of time. Rebellion, however, brought the curse, and so for now, there is hardship and there is tribulation. It is hard; if it were not, we would not look to God, would we? "In this world, you will have tribulation, but take heart, I have overcome the world," says

Jesus Christ (John 16:33b). Of this you can be certain, the one who is in control of your life is completely trustworthy.

Maybe the LORD is not calling you to a land that you have not known (or maybe He is), but undoubtedly, you are facing (or will face) a change, a trial, a tribulation, or a heartache. It is in these moments we are faced with a choice. Will we trust in Him who is trustworthy, regardless of how it appears or feels, or will we submit to unbelief, fear, and panic? At times, it may feel like this – I know you brought me here, but where are you? Of course, He is right there with us, working all things together for good. When we cannot immediately discern just what that is and we feel like we are completely in the dark, we must, through faith, continue to trust in Him. Our God is faithful, and our shield is our faith in *His* faithfulness!

I cannot emphasize it enough. Anchor yourself to the Word of God. If you do not take up the full armor of God, which includes the sword of the Spirit, you will not have done everything you can to stand, and you will not stand. We have a powerful enemy working hard to deceive and attempting to dethrone Jesus Christ as LORD of our lives. Take heart, He who is in you is greater than he who is in the world, and we have been given the weapons necessary to be successful in this war raging against our devotion to Christ and our fruitfulness. Tell me though, what good is a sword that you do not use in the heat of battle or that you do not even pick up? We are engaged in all-out warfare, and we must treat it as such. There is good news, however. The battle belongs to the LORD, so do not be afraid, for those who are with us are more than those who are with them (II Kings 6:16).

We know that we have whatever we ask for if it is within the will of the Father (I John 5:14-15). The LORD desires our faith. In fact, it is impossible to please God without it (Hebrews 11:6a). So ask, and you will receive. If you find yourself lacking in this department, tell Him. Please LORD, increase my faith; help me trust you more. Then brace yourself (in Him) for trial. The tested genuineness of your faith will be tested by fire and is more precious than gold, and it will be found to result in praise and glory and honor at the revelation of Jesus Christ (see I Peter 1:7). So, count it all joy, my brothers and sisters, when you meet trials of various kinds, for you know the testing of your faith produces steadfastness, which is the quality of being resolutely or dutifully firm and unwavering (see James 1:2-3).

The more victories He works through my frailty and weaknesses, the stronger my faith and trust in Him becomes. What is He asking of you today? Will you put one foot in front of the other and trust Him for ALL the rest? There is a tremendous amount of freedom found in trusting the LORD with all your heart.

The tendency is to try to make sense of our circumstances through relying on our own understanding. It is a trap! Do not fall for it! One reason we want to understand and make sense of things is because we think if we can understand it, we can control it and maybe not be subject to feeling dependent or unstable. The truth is we lack even the ability to comprehend all that God is doing, so the things that we (and those we love) go through will not likely make an ounce of sense. They are not necessarily supposed to. These trials are not designed to help us understand; they are designed to help us learn to trust in Him even though we do not understand.

I love this scripture: We do not know what to do, but our eyes are on you (II Chronicles 20:12). As long as we trust God with our whole heart and do not lean on our own flawed understanding but in all our ways acknowledge Him, He will, without a doubt, keep our paths straight. I have seen it over and over and over again as I am sure many of you have! We serve a loving and totally faithful God. Hallelujah!

- You keep him in perfect peace whose mind is stayed on you, because he trusts in you (Isaiah 26:3).
- Trust in Him at all times, O people. Pour out your heart before Him. God is a refuge for us (Psalm 62:8).
- They cried out to God in the battle, and He granted their urgent plea because they trusted in Him (I Chronicles 5:20).
- And those who know your name put their trust in you for you, O LORD, have not forsaken those who seek you (Psalm 9:10).

Wait on the LORD

Wait for the LORD!
Be strong and let your heart take courage.
Wait for the LORD!
Psalm 27:14

TRUSTING IN THE LORD and waiting on the LORD go hand in hand. In fact, when we wait on the LORD, we are actively putting into practice the trust we have in Him. By actively waiting on Him, we demonstrate that we believe He is who He says He is and that He does what He says He will do.

If you have ever waited on the LORD, you know this is not an act for the faint of heart. In my experience, the LORD comes in at the eleventh hour and not often before. Of course, this makes perfect sense because hope that is seen is not hope. For who hopes for what he sees? But if we hope for what we do not see, we wait for it with patience (Romans 8:24b-25). It is not hard to trust the LORD when everything is going right. The true testing materializes when everything seems to be going wrong.

Often, our limited vision will cause our will and our timing to be far different from that of God's will and His timing. He knows everything. We know next to nothing, and that is a generous statement. If we really trusted the LORD with our whole heart, we would be doing a lot more waiting and a lot less scurrying to *make things happen*. You may have heard the phrase "God helps those who help themselves." There is nothing biblical about this – Nothing. Are we given responsibilities by the Father? Sure, unquestionably. I am not suggesting that we sit around and do absolutely nothing, but I will say this; there is much busyness that amounts to just that – Absolutely nothing.

When God revealed to me that I would leave one state for another, I began to try to "make it happen." It was frustrating when all my efforts brought me to a dead end. However, as soon as time entered into His timing, the plans and details came to fruition effortlessly. His yoke really is easy, and His burden really is light if we would stop trying to do it on our own and learn to wait on Him.

The next time He revealed that we would leave one state for another, I definitely kept the matter in mind, but I did not focus on accomplishing this. I knew that in His time and in His way, He would guide and direct my steps to perform His will. It was not up to me to make it happen, and there is so much freedom found in that truth.

In the last chapter, I spoke of moving into our "own" apartment. This would not have transpired if I had taken matters into my own hands by accepting the offer I was sure the LORD did not want me to accept. Even though my direction was not revealed until the very last day, waiting on the LORD to show me where He wanted us to go was essential. There was certainly a temptation to become impatient as I waited for His direction and intervention, but His grace was sufficient, and great is His faithfulness.

As you recall, I heard a city and state one morning as I was waking up. In the following months, I would get several more confirmations as well as a wave of peace about this next move. In addition, the arrangements were nearly effortless. All the details were smoothly worked out by the LORD, and our bus tickets were ordered. God will accomplish that which He wills. Too often, we make the mistake of trying to do more than God has asked of us or we try to get ahead of Him. Moving at our own pace, we then become out of sync and find ourselves walking, or even running, outside of His will all because we struggle so hard to be still (cease striving) and know that He is God!

As I was waking up one morning in this new apartment, something interesting happened. Words began shooting clearly through my mind. It was the gospel. Write it down, I thought. I took a 5 x 7 index card and began to write. God had given me an articulation of the gospel in simple but clear terms, and it fit perfectly on the card. I then thought, wouldn't it be something if I could put a short testimony on the back testifying to the hope I found in Jesus Christ. To my surprise, those words began to come too. I then realized I had my own version (given by God) of a Bible tract, and it was personal, and it was concise. As long as it stays bathed in prayer, it continues to be a powerful, well-received, and effective way of scattering seeds.

We stayed in this apartment for seven months, and as we got closer to our moving day, the LORD provided consistent reassurance and peace about it. I found great comfort in Psalm 121 as I began to more fully grasp that my help comes from the LORD, maker of heaven and earth. Nothing is too hard for Him. Knowing that the LORD, himself, is my keeper was (and is) remarkably comforting to me. One week prior to our move, I felt prompted to turn the radio on, and this is what I heard; I am paving the way for you. Just stand back and watch what I am about to do for you. It brought tears to my eyes. It reminds me of Exodus 14:13-14, which He has used often in my journey. And Moses said to the people, fear not, stand firm, and see the salvation of the LORD, which He will work for you today. The LORD will fight for you, and you have only to be silent. He truly is the God of all comfort!

Moving day arrived, and we boarded a bus at midnight. We spent the next thirty-six hours en route to an unknown land with no plan. Sound familiar? Just as was evident on the last two incredibly long bus rides with active children (now 3 and 4 years old), God's grace was super sufficient, and He kindly covered us completely in it. We landed two days later at noon. I had no clue what was in store, but I was confident that I was walking out the will of God, and I could rely on Him to guide me (I still did not use a cellphone at this point). I felt a strong, unwavering trust in Him, and there were no tears shed this time. He kept me in this state of patient trust as I looked forward to how He would work, and I felt so much peace, which was truly a gift.

As I stood outside the Greyhound station and looked around, I saw an old stadium and not much of anything else. I sighed a little bit. Then, I threw on my backpack and tossed the bags onto the stroller. I began to put one foot in front of the other and continued to pray without ceasing. We were all hungry, so that was the first stop. The LORD had provided us several hundred dollars for this adventure, for which I was thankful. I have seen Him provide just as easily without the use of money, but that is what He decided upon at this time.

After lunch, we continued walking, and we came upon a Salvation Army. That would not be the answer; there was a waiting list. As we came out of there, I noticed I had been walking alongside Grace (Street)! I literally laughed out loud with joy. I sure was walking alongside Grace. Thank you, Father.

It was now 4 p.m. I felt exhaustion beginning to set in, and we were all worn out from the long trip. With the money I had, I could probably get a hotel room for a couple of nights and make phone calls from the room in the morning. The problem was finding a hotel that would take cash only, no credit card, and no ID – A nearly impossible find. However, impossible is easy for God. I asked Him, "LORD, would it be all right to use this money to try to find a room?" To my relief, I felt a peaceful yes.

Immediately following this, I realized we were a block away from a well-known hotel chain. I thought, there is no way they will give me a room with no card and no ID, but nothing is impossible for God, so we headed inside. It soon became apparent He did not lead me there to rent a room but for information. The guy behind the desk could not, in fact, give me a room, but he had been homeless at one point and knew exactly which hotel I should try. He even knew which bus I should take to get there. He said it was a sketchy part of town, but I knew it would be. The LORD protects. In peace I will both lie down and sleep; for you alone, O LORD, make me dwell in safety (Psalm 4:8). So, after he offered us chips and water on the house, we were on our way *somewhere*. It was a good feeling as opposed to walking around, what can seem, aimlessly.

We arrived around 6 p.m. Initially, he said yes to cash but no way without an ID. Sigh. I was not expecting that, but I prayed and resolved there must be a different plan. However, the Holy Spirit moved in the way that only He can. The guy made a quick phone call and, all of a sudden, we had a room! Our Great God had faithfully guided every step of the way. It was a great relief for all three of us to walk into that tiny room despite the weird little bed and obviously crazy high neighbors. My children and I were praising God with hands lifted high!

My 4 and 5-year-old have been blessed in wisdom far beyond their years. They realize our stability comes from Christ alone. All other ground is sinking sand and subject to change at a moment's notice. They have been given the grace to understand on a practical level that God is with us wherever we are and wherever we go, and He is faithful to us. They have been given the extraordinary opportunity to learn firsthand that we do not find our stability in people, places, or things. Our stability comes from God alone. We feel secure because He is with us, and He is for us. One of our many favorite verses is Deuteronomy 31:6. Be strong and courageous. Do not be afraid for the LORD your God goes with you. He will never leave you nor forsake you.

As often as their environment has changed, their childlike confidence and trust in the LORD has not wavered because their temperament and their security has not rested upon the temporal and the fleeting but upon the constant presence of God. The scenery may change, the people may change, but our God stays the same. With God's grace and favor poured over them in abundance, they possess a wisdom deeply rooted that far exceeds that of many adults. It is God who has led us from place to place according to His will, and His grace is more than sufficient to live the life He has called each of us to live, down to the smallest of details. He has even kept their daytime and nighttime routines completely intact.

While this journey has been unique and unconventional, my children have benefited tremendously in the ways in which they know God, believe God, and trust God. Jesus Christ is our life, and our conversations are centered around eternal things. We spend precious time in worship and prayer, and they will quote scripture with magnificent timing. They also enjoy acting out stories from the Bible as they play. He is their peace. He is their stability. He is their trust, and it shows. They shine His light wherever we go.

Just recently, a woman we were meeting for the first time said, "I don't know what it is about your children, but they are radiant, and you are doing a wonderful job." I said, "Actually, it is Christ. It is Jesus Christ." This was not at all unusual to hear because everywhere we go, people comment on how joyful and peaceful my children seem to be, especially in light of our circumstances. I would suggest that it is those very circumstances which are molding them in such a way that God is most glorified through them. They are sensitive to the things of God and to the things which are not. There is a desensitization running rampant in our world today, of which they know nothing. They are well adjusted, compassionate, and kind, and God gets all the glory. I have spent many hours in prayer for *all* of my children, and I am so thankful for His grace and His faithfulness.

After a good night of sleep, we were given the gift of a beautifully relaxing day in the presence of the LORD, for which I was so grateful. There were no land lines at the hotel, so we set out to find a safe place to make phone calls. As I was looking around, God laid it on my heart to take a day to unwind, and He led us to a beautiful river. We spent time in nature with God, and He replenished our souls.

The following morning, God led me to a church that would break its COVID rules and allow me to come inside to use the phone. At first, they would not allow it, but when God moves, so do people. We were there for several hours, mostly waiting on return phone calls, and it was not going well. I was beginning to get discouraged, but the LORD reminded me that He told me to come here, and there was, indeed, a plan; I must keep trusting with a thankful heart. He helped me extinguish the fiery darts as I continued to wait. Finally, I was given a number I could try in the morning. There was no verification that it would mean a place to stay, but it was not nothing. The next morning, I called the number, and she was excited to tell me that I had been accepted. She then gave me the address of a hotel where we would stay for the next six months.

Almost immediately, the LORD would lead us to the church He had picked out for us, and He used my 4-year-old daughter to do so. We were riding on a bus when "out of the blue" my daughter, who could not see out of the window, said, "I want to go to church!" It was in that very moment, my head turned to catch a glimpse of what would become our church for a season. It was a loving congregation of people, who welcomed us with open arms and lots of love. They would also play a crucial role in our lives in this upcoming season of waiting and testing.

The hotel and the area surrounding would prove to be an area in need of the truth of the gospel and perfect territory for scattering seeds and prayers of intercession. There was no shortage of the hurting and homeless in bondage, desperately in need of the hope found in Christ alone.

As we approached the three-month mark at this hotel, I had a meeting with the caseworker, and it was my understanding that I had been given a thirty-day extension in that meeting. That impression would turn out to be false, a huge miscommunication. The staff would appear at my door at that three-month mark and say to me, "Your exit date is tomorrow. I hope you have made plans because you cannot stay here." You can imagine my shock and dismay. I explained that I was under the impression I had received an extension. The response? "We are sorry to hear that, but you have got to go." I pleaded, "Is there any way to get an extension at this point?" The answer was no. I felt somewhat discouraged, as is the tendency when the rug gets pulled out from under you. In this case, it was the roof from over mine and my children's heads being pulled. However, I was confident of this – My God, who loves us perfectly, was in complete and total control. A friend of mine would say it this way: All my circumstances come from God.

This was a surprise to me, but it was no surprise to God. He knew this was coming, and He already had it all worked out, even though it did not seem like it. I asked the staff why they did not give me a few more days' notice. Apparently, it was protocol to receive five days' notice, but somehow my case had fallen through the cracks. This was also from God. This was an important test. Would I continue to trust in Him completely? Would I patiently and thankfully wait for Him? Yes, by the grace of God, I would. I poured out my heart to Him and said, "LORD, I do not know what is going on, but I accept it, and I ask you to direct my steps. Your sovereignty is a huge comfort to me. Thank you for your presence. Thank you for your peace." One of the many scriptures He used to comfort me in this time was Isaiah 40:11. He will tend His flock like a shepherd. He will gather the lambs in His arms. He will carry them in His bosom and *gently lead those that are with young* (italics added). It was not the first time He comforted me with this verse, and it would not be the last.

I spent that evening in prayer and praise and packing. My journal entry that evening goes like this: I just need to keep walking and keep trusting. I do not need to seek the solution. I need to seek You, the possessor of the solution. You are my help. You are my refuge. I am not afraid of bad news, and I will not be greatly shaken. As I put my daughter to bed, she recited this verse from Colossians: Set your mind on things above, not on things of earth. Thank you, my child, for helping me stay heavenly minded. It is strangely hard to do when faced with circumstances such as these, but I know that I totally trust you, LORD, and I know you will guide me and continue to provide. I love you. I feel as if I will be singing your mercies are new every morning. Great is your faithfulness! I am so thankful you are in our boat, Jesus. I know this storm will calm as soon as you give the word. Give me your strength and your wisdom. You have never failed me, and you never will.

The next morning I wrote this: Good morning, Father. I am thinking quite a bit about the events of the day. Knowing we cannot stay here tonight, I wonder what your plan is, but I need to stop wondering and just walk and trust. I am so grateful for your presence. To walk through this mess without you would be unfathomable. Thank you for being with me wherever I go.

I then began my scripture reading for the morning, and the first one said, I will lead the blind in a way that they do not know, in paths they have not known. I will guide them. I will turn the darkness before them into light, the rough places into level ground. These are the things that I do, and I do not forsake them. Thank you, Father. Then I read, your steadfast love surrounds me because I trust you. Then, I could not believe it! Sure enough, the scripture in one of my devotions was Lamentations 3:21-23! Your mercies are new every morning. Great is your faithfulness! Then I turned on the radio while I got ready, and a song played, singing great is your faithfulness! It is just like I wrote last night – That I would be singing your praise for your mercies are new every morning. Great is your faithfulness!

I did not know what to do, but I kept my eyes on Him. The caseworker came to my door. She felt sad for us but reiterated that her hands were tied. With confidence, I assured her all would be well; my God is with me. I told her of my plans to go to an office downtown to attempt to get help finding shelter for the night.

The thirty-minute bus ride was notably peaceful as I was comforted by the nearness of the LORD. It was a cold, gray, overcast morning, and it began to pour rain. In addition, my children were both sick. I was tempted to become bitter and complain about the sickness and the rain, but by the grace of God, I did not. Instead, I praised Him all the more. The minute we got off of the bus, the rain slowed down to nothing, and it did not rain on us. He led me on a different path than we had been before, and it was one beautiful moment after another as He comforted me through this trial.

As we walked, I sang praise and thanked God for the intimacy in this uncertain time. I had every reason to rejoice in these circumstances for my God was *noticeably* with me. I took courage for the hand of the LORD my God was on me (Ezra 7:28).

When we got to the office, I explained my situation to the woman at the desk and asked if I could use the phone. My children and I then used the restroom, and by the time we came out, she said, "The caseworker at the hotel just sent me a message. She wants you to call her." That's odd, I thought. I called her, and I almost could not believe my ears. The extension that was altogether impossible and out of the question . . . had been granted. Wow God! Wow! I did not see that one coming. It was miraculous. He had instantaneously calmed the storm, and as we walked out those doors, the sky above had begun to clear up as well; the sun began to shine through the beautiful clouds against a blue sky, and I stood in awe. This detour would prove to be a useful and powerful testimony to share and proclaim the goodness and faithfulness of God with my neighbors. His power truly shines most brilliantly in all of my weaknesses.

Over the course of the next thirty days, the LORD impressed upon me several times (through scripture); do not fear, only believe. I still had no clue what to do. It seemed I had made every phone call I could and exhausted all my options. I was certainly talking to the LORD about it, but there was no concrete direction that I could discern. He seemed to be silent. I surely wanted Him to clue me in, but that was just not happening. However, I knew that He was still working, and He was still working in me in many ways.

The book of Esther is a good example of this sort of thing. The name of God is not mentioned one time in the book of Esther. We do not see God speak throughout Esther either. It seems as if He might be silent or even absent, but if we take a step back and look at the entire story, the big picture, we see His mighty hand all over the place, working things out according to His purpose. His presence and sovereign orchestrating power is undeniable.

At the end of thirty days, I still did not know what I was supposed to do. It seemed an incredibly hopeless situation with no opportunities in sight. I was given the charge by God not to accept any government assistance by way of food stamps, housing, etc. So, from the time we fled for refuge, never did I apply for any of these things at the shock, and often disapproval, from others.

Every time someone would bring it up again, I would inquire of the LORD, and every time (many times), He would lead me to one of the many scriptures warning, do not go to Egypt for help (Egypt in this case being the government). Do not go to Egypt. Know for a certainty that I have warned you this day (Jeremiah 42:19). Ah stubborn children, declares the LORD, who carry out a plan but not mine and who make an alliance but not of my Spirit that they may add sin to sin who set out to go down to Egypt without asking for my direction to take refuge in the protection of Pharaoh and to seek shelter in the shadow of Egypt. Therefore, shall the protection of Pharaoh turn to your shame and the shelter in the shadow of Egypt to your humiliation (Isaiah 30:1-3). Woe to those who go down to Egypt for help and rely on horses . . . The Egyptians are men and not God, and their horses are flesh and not spirit (Isaiah 31:1, 3). This did not happen just a couple of times, but every single time I inquired, "LORD, do I sign up for government assistance?" The answer has always been, no, backed up by scripture.

It seems to me that this call on my life to abstain from receiving government handouts/assistance has been but a foretaste of the call that will come upon all Christians everywhere in the not too distant future.

The night before leaving the hotel, I wrote in my journal: It feels like my body is going to collapse (the kiddos and I are sick right now), but you are keeping me going, giving me your strength. Thank you. I started to pack a little bit when I got a call from a caseworker with no good news, but it did not get me down. I know you will put us exactly where you want us to be. As soon as I hung up the phone, I heard the tail end of what someone said on the radio. "Just keep trusting Him one small step at a time." Beautiful! My God is in control. Thank you for uplifting me right when I need it. My help does not come from man. My help comes from You, the maker of heaven and earth. I trust you. Thy will be done.

I felt confident that I was still walking within the will of God; that I was obeying His voice despite opposition; and that no decisions had been made, big or small, that I did not first lay before the LORD. I had seen Him come through for me so miraculously time and time again, and I have read about Him coming through for others in the Bible time and time again. My faith felt strong, but my feelings felt weak. It was another time of humbling, and it was not easy to go through.

Thankfully, the LORD directed the church body to step in and help us. Initially, they put us up in a hotel for five days. Then, after putting their heads together, it was decided we could stay in a room at the church where we would have access to a bathroom, kitchen, and a large gym. In the days leading up to our departure from the hotel, God was faithfully strengthening me with encouraging scriptures of comfort, as evidenced by my journal. For whatever was written in the former days was written for our instruction, that through endurance and through the encouragement of the scriptures, we might have hope (Romans 15:4). He truly is the God of endurance and encouragement. Still, this was a weird time for me.

For the first several days, my pride did not want the church to *have to* step in and help me, even though that is what God had ordained. Because others knew so little of my story and next to nothing of my personal conversations with God, it would be easy for some to look down on me and conclude from our situation that I must be doing something wrong or that my choices must not be from God. It came in the form of words from friends, but I was under attack. We do not wrestle against flesh and blood, so I cried out to God all the more. "LORD, show me if I am wrong! But if I am not, and if I have been hearing you right, please give me the strength to stand. Give me forgiveness for others, and help me to love them, especially when it is difficult." I had my own feelings to deal with on top of misunderstanding from others, and it was such a difficult time. He told me to be careful. Be quiet. Do not fear and do not let your heart faint because of these . . . If you are not firm in faith, you will not be firm at all (Isaiah 7).

Fighting much discouragement, I kept reminding myself of what I knew to be true. I know God called me here; I know He loves me with an everlasting love; I know He has never failed me; I know He will never leave me nor forsake me; I know He is with me wherever I go; I know it is He who fights my battles; I know that He is so much bigger than any "giant" I will ever face; and I know He is a God who makes a way when there is no way. So, I clung to Him, and I clung to His Word, and I continued to praise Him in the storm, even though He had not seen fit to reveal anything to me.

My journal throughout these days of trial is page after page of scriptures, to which God led me, in order to strengthen me, encourage me, reassure me, and carry me through this extremely difficult time. It is all completely relevant, and each day's scriptures fit perfectly with the thoughts, emotions, and challenges I faced. How He does that, how He orchestrates His Word so perfectly, I will never understand. His thoughts are very deep and how vast is the sum of them. I am amazed by the Word of God and the way He desires to use it in our lives as we immerse ourselves in it. I stand in awe. His timing is impeccable.

One of the scriptures He led me to the night before moving into the church was I Peter 4:12, which says, Beloved, do not be surprised at the fiery trial when it comes upon you to test you as though something strange were happening to you. I needed this gentle reminder because it did feel like something strange was happening to me. He also said through scripture, and after you have suffered a little while, the God of all grace who has called you to His eternal glory in Christ will Himself restore, confirm, strengthen, and establish you (I Peter 5:10). I love that, and that is just what He would eventually do because He is the lifter of my head. But you, O LORD, are a shield about me, the glory, and the lifter of my head (Psalm 3:3).

The first night in the church, I would get access to worship music. For several hours, I would sing praises to God through many tears, and His presence would overwhelm me with His joy and peace. I repented from the obvious pride and need for the approval of others, which was still hidden inside of me – A truth revealed through the trial. One of the many purposes of a trial is to reveal what is in us. It is through that pressure and squeezing that our underlying sin can surface and, thereby, be dealt with. That night, I wrote: Thank you for the worship music tonight, the tears, your comfort, your presence, LORD. I do not like what I am going through, and I do not like being in the dark, but I trust you with all of my heart, and I praise your glorious name in this storm. Give me wisdom and courage and help me to be okay with step-by-step instructions. I came across this tonight; help in the wilderness is not available through man, only your divine intervention. Manna comes in daily doses only.

The second day at the church, I felt as if I ought to be making phone calls, but one of the things God told me that morning (twice) during my time spent with Him was that I needed to be still (cease striving) and know that He is God. I would like to say it was not a struggle, but it was definitely an internal struggle with my own feelings of what I *should be doing* as well as the possible judgment that might fall on me from others (whether that was real or a fabrication of my mind). There it was again, pride and the desire for approval up against obedience to the LORD's command to be still and to sit at His feet, seeking Him. By the grace of God, obedience won, and it was a truly relaxing day, in which I simply sought His face and trusted Him for everything else.

The next day, He would urge me to make one phone call. An hour later, I would receive a return call, and a voice on the other end said they had approved me to go back to the hotel we came from for another sixty days. Wow. Thank you, LORD. My faith was stronger now, and I had learned some invaluable lessons. Additionally, what would I have accomplished the previous day if I had frantically kept myself busy with trying to make something happen other than dis-obedience followed by missing out on the calm and rest that God Al-mighty had planned to give me? How many of us are missing out on the delightful reward the LORD wants to give us by way of rest in His presence simply because our pride tells us we should be busy doing something? Isaiah 30:15 comes to mind. For thus said the LORD God, the Holy One of Israel, in returning and rest you shall be saved. In quietness and in trust shall be your strength, but you were unwilling. Waiting on the LORD may not be easy, but it is so worth it.

A few days after we moved back to the hotel, my children and I went on a prayer walk. At the end of this walk, I asked the LORD to lead me to someone searching for Him and asked Him to prepare their heart to receive one of my gospel cards. A block later, he did just that. He pointed a woman out, known for her services, who I had seen around previously. I said, "Excuse me, hello, may I give this to you?" I handed her a card and $10. She burst into tears and talked for twenty minutes about how good God is. It was her birthday, and she said, "Please God, just send someone who will give me $10." She was obviously overwhelmed by the joy of His presence, and so was I. Though she had lost her way, she knew Jesus, and she knew He knew her. God spoke to me through that woman, saying, you are exactly where you are supposed to be. You are out here for this very reason, and it was a beautiful assurance. She went on to quote a verse my children had just memorized, which we were recently saying often. The LORD is my strength and my shield. My heart trusts in Him, and He helps me (Psalm 27:8). Incredible. How often have I gone out into the trenches with the prayer that God would use me to be a blessing to others and how often that blessing shoots right back at me. I left that conversation so encouraged by and so in love with my Savior. I would also pray intently for this woman to be freed from the bondage for good. Interesting enough, I never saw her again. My hope is that our prayers were answered.

As the end of that sixty days was approaching, I still had no idea what to do next. My church did say we could go back there if we needed to, and the LORD granted me humility to gratefully ask for and accept that help. I was totally grateful the last time, but my pride tried to keep me upset about it. This time was not like that. In addition, as I listened to a sermon about the crossing of the Red Sea, God spoke assurance to my heart. It seemed as if God had led the Israelites straight into a dead end, right? In my own life, it seemed He had brought me out of "Egypt" and led me through the wilderness straight into a dead end. Therefore, I knew in my heart, and was confident, that it meant He was about to part the waters. If I would only wait on Him to move, He had it all worked out.

I heard about a transitional home in the area which offered an 18-month program. I tried to get in touch with them many times, but I always got a busy signal. My pastor did email to inquire about a spot, but there was no space available. I had pretty much given up on this place by now. However, as I pulled a bunch of out-of-state phone numbers from my backpack, I came across the number to this home, and I heard that still, small voice say, "Call it." I did not expect it to work; I really did not. When a kind woman answered, I could not believe it. To my utter shock, she said, "Well yes, I think we do have room." My jaw dropped, and I was elated. I especially liked the verse on their website, obviously: Under His wings you will find refuge (Psalm 91:4). There was just one obstacle. It cost $600/month, and I had no income. I knew, however, that if this was the will of God, He would provide. There was no doubt about that. He is the God who makes a way when there is no way. It took a couple of weeks to get the application and interview completed, but I was accepted. God then provided the first month's rent followed by the second, then the third, then the fourth, fifth, sixth, seventh, eighth, ninth, and tenth, and I have been using that time to write this book. Astounding.

God put the writing of a book on my heart several years ago, but I have been waiting on His timing to do so. We had been in this home for a couple of weeks when the LORD began to impress upon my heart and mind that the time to write was approaching. As I laid in bed one night curiously pondering this massive undertaking, I inquired of the LORD. What should it be about? In what format? Which content? To which I sensed He responded, tell them what I have taught you. I felt overwhelmed at this notion, but He began to put chapter titles in my mind, so I wrote them down, and I started writing the next day. It certainly is God who works in us to will and to work for His good pleasure (Philippians 2:13).

Once we begin to internally grasp exactly from where our help comes, from the maker of heaven and earth, waiting on Him becomes a little easier. His sovereignty is a great comfort to me. Chances are, you will come against opposition and misunderstanding from others as you wait upon the LORD, especially in our culture infiltrated with the illusion of self-sufficiency. It may seem to those around you that you are not doing all you should or could be doing. You may even be told something like, God only helps those who help themselves. Stand firm. Do not be discouraged. If He is telling you to wait . . . wait! Those who wait for the LORD will not be put to shame. To the contrary, those who wait on the LORD will mount up with wings like an eagle.

There are many ways we wait upon the LORD. We wait on the LORD as we long to put on the immortal to enjoy perfection in His presence forever. We wait on the LORD to reveal a certain path we ought to take or to give us direction. We wait on the LORD for healing, both physical and emotional. We wait on the LORD to reveal His will for our lives. We wait on the LORD as we lift up our prayers and petitions for others. We wait on the LORD to calm a storm in His time. You may be waiting on the return of a prodigal or maybe you are waiting on Him to move in the midst of a broken or difficult relationship. There are an endless number of ways we may find ourselves waiting upon the LORD. This is where praise and perseverance come into play, which I will cover more in depth in the next chapter.

He does not immediately fix all of our problems; some of those are for our good. However, when He moves in an impossible situation in a way no human ever could have, you cannot help but be struck by awe, and you find that it was, indeed, worth the wait.

- I wait for the LORD. My soul waits, and in His Word I hope. My soul waits for the LORD more than watchman for the morning (Psalm 130:5-6).
- The LORD is good to those who wait for Him, to the soul who seeks Him (Lamentations 3:25).
- Our soul waits for the LORD. He is our help and our shield. For our heart is glad in Him because we trust in His holy name (Psalm 33:20-21).
- Be still before the LORD and wait patiently for Him. Fret not yourself over the one who prospers in his way (Psalm 37:7).

- But as for me, I will look to the Lord; I will wait for the God of my salvation; my God will hear me (Micah 7:7).

CHAPTER FOUR

Praise God in the Storm – For He is Faithful

For you have been my help,
and in the shadow of your wings,
I will sing for joy.
My soul clings to you; your right hand upholds me.
Psalm 63:7-8

TO TRUST IN THE LORD and wait upon Him in a way that is honoring of Him, we must remain in a posture of thankfulness and praise deep within our hearts. If we find ourselves grumbling as we wait upon the LORD, we need to repent and quickly return, taking every thought captive to obey Christ. We cannot do this apart from an intimate relationship with Him because it is His faithful, steadfast love and character which will produce the deep gratitude within us. It is a firm grasp on our own depravity and, therefore, the amazing grace of salvation which will cause us to praise Him even in the midst of pain and trial.

A beautiful thing takes place when we choose to praise Him in the storm. His presence will bring peace that cannot be explained, and fears will diminish and disappear completely. Do not be anxious about anything, but in everything by prayer and supplication with thanksgiving let your requests be made known to God. And the peace of God, which surpasses all understanding, will guard your hearts and your minds in Christ Jesus (Philippians 4:6-7). This is one of the ways we can set our minds on things above, not on things of earth (Colossians 3:2) for to set the mind on the flesh is death, but to set the mind on the Spirit is life and peace (Romans 8:6).

Our circumstances are temporal; they will not last and should not be our focus. I do not say that flippantly as I am sure many of you are in the midst of or are about to enter into various painful, heartbreaking, and difficult circumstances. You may be facing storms in which you are surrounded by darkness, and it seems as if you are going to drown. You feel weak, you feel vulnerable, and you are exhausted from the struggle against the wind and the waves. In addition, it seems as if the Lord Jesus is fast asleep. Be assured, He is not. He who watches over you neither slumbers nor sleeps (Psalm 121:4). So, take heart and cling to Him and cling to His Word. Lift up your voice in praise and worship and adoration for who He is, and you will be blessed. You will, indeed, be blessed. Your circumstance may not change, but your perspective will, and you will be blessed with His presence and His peace, which surpasses all understanding. Draw near to God, and He will draw near to you (James 4:8a).

Many believers have fallen prey to this notion, this lie, that once we decide to follow Christ, our lives should be easy. Nowhere in God's Word does it say we will have it easy. In fact, we are promised, instead, to have lives full of suffering, trials, and tribulation, not because God has it out for us, but because we live in a fallen world. In addition, we do not learn very much when we have it easy. If we do not already know better (sometimes even if we do), we begin to think we do not need God. We begin to think we can handle it, and we are deceived into believing we have it all under control.

Our pride runs rampant if not kept in check. It is at the very core of all sin. What was the cause of Lucifer's demise? In one word – Pride. To think we know better than God, to think we somehow make better decisions than He does is, of course, ludicrous. To think my limited vision and understanding is even comparable to the one Sovereign God, Creator of all, is insanity. He is the Potter; we are but a lump of clay. Woe to him who strives with Him who formed him, a pot among earthen pots! Does the clay say to Him who forms it, "What are you making? Or your work has no handles?" (Isaiah 45:9). You turn things upside down! Shall the potter be regarded as the clay that the thing made should say of its maker, "He did not make me"; or the thing formed say of him who formed it, "He has no understanding?" (Isaiah 29:16).

It is through our suffering, trials, and tribulations that we are shaped and molded; it is where the genuineness of our faith is tested; it is where we learn how to trust God; it is where we are humbled; and it is where God works out His own divine, unseen purposes within the spiritual realm as we see evident in the case of Job. The possibilities of why we are faced with hardship and trial are as limitless as God's thoughts and intentions.

He (Jesus Christ) learned obedience through what He suffered (Hebrews 5:8), and if Jesus Christ, himself, was called to suffer, why wouldn't we? You may think . . . but didn't He suffer so that we do not have to? The answer is yes, when the time comes to enter into forever, but we still live in a broken, fallen world at present. Indeed, all who desire to live a godly life in Christ Jesus will be persecuted (II Timothy 3:12). For what credit is it if when you sin and are beaten for it, you endure, but if when you do good and suffer for it, you endure, this is a gracious thing in the sight of God for to this you have been called, because Christ also suffered for you, leaving you an example, so that you might follow in His steps (I Peter 2:20-21).

Once we enter the eternal realm, we will be without suffering, trial, and tribulation. In fact, He will wipe away every tear from our eyes and death shall be no more, neither shall there be mourning nor crying nor pain! What a beautiful inheritance! However, too many of us have given into some grand illusion that we should have heaven on earth now. It is not wrong or unreasonable to long for the perfect, for in this tent we groan, longing to put on our heavenly dwelling. God has put eternity into a man's heart for a reason, but He makes all things beautiful in His time.

Fortunately, we are not left to suffer alone or without reprieve through the comfort of God. For as we share abundantly in Christ's sufferings, so through Christ we share in comfort too. Blessed be the God and Father of our Lord Jesus Christ, the Father of Mercies and God of all comfort, who comforts us in all our affliction (II Corinthians 1:5, 3). Paul goes on to say in verses 8-10, we were so utterly burdened beyond our strength that we despaired of life itself. Indeed, we felt we had received the sentence of death, but that was to make us rely not on ourselves but on God who raises the dead. He delivered us from such a deadly peril, and He will deliver us. On Him we have set our hope that He will deliver us again. *But that was to make us rely not on ourselves but on God!* In Romans 5, we are told that we can rejoice in our suffering for it produces endurance, which produces character, which produces hope, which does not put us to shame.

What I have come to learn is that my deepest joys and greatest intimacies have been enjoyed in the midst of my greatest trials and heartbreaks. This would not be true had I not been actively seeking His face, but there is a depth to my intimacy with God in the midst of suffering, which brings indescribable joy and inner peace. In fact, it is so incredible that I would rather suffer with Christ by my side than live a care-free, pain-free life in which He felt the least bit distant. May we spend less time asking God to deliver us from the pain and suffering which He has allowed and more time seeking His comforting presence, strength, and grace to endure it.

In Job Ch. 1, he loses his children, his servants, and his animals in one fell swoop through no fault of his own – Devastating! His response? Mourning and worship. He fell on his face and worshiped. When his wife encouraged him to turn his back on God, his response was, "Shall we receive good from God and shall we not receive disaster?" Oh, how we can learn from the faithfulness of Job. For I consider that the sufferings of this present time are not worth comparing with the glory that is to be revealed to us (Romans 8:18). Our suffering is limited. Our resurrection is eternal. For this light momentary affliction is preparing for us an eternal weight of glory beyond all comparison as we look not to the things that are seen but to the things that are unseen. For the things that are seen are transient, but the things that are unseen are eternal (II Corinthians 4:17-18).

I do not say any of this to disregard real and painful emotions, namely the heartache and grief, any number of you may be experiencing in these very moments. Your emotions were created by God, and there is a real period of grieving we must go through when our hearts feel like they have been physically shattered within us. I am no stranger to this deep, guttural pain, and some grief never goes away. However, we can, indeed, rejoice in our sorrow as we look to our God for His intimate comfort.

The separation from five of my children has been unfathomably painful, and it is an underlying sorrow and anguish that is always there. My heart breaks because I grieve that loss so tremendously. I grieve the inability to hold them, to comfort them, to listen to them, to encourage them, and to teach them all the many wonderful things the LORD has been teaching me. Knowing they are experiencing sickness, suffering, and any manner of trial and heartache that comes with this life, and I cannot be there for them is something I can barely stomach. As a mother who deeply loves her children and always has, there is no way I could ever adequately describe to anyone the depth or complexity of my painful emotions when it comes to the absence of my children. My longing to hold them and show them my affection and love for them has hurt immensely for a long time. I grieve their presence so terribly that words cannot adequately describe my sorrow; but I rejoice in my God, the Healer of all wounds, who turns ashes into beauty and curses into blessings. I lift their precious lives up to my Father in heaven, and with praise on my lips for who He is to me, I entrust them into His loving, everlasting arms to redeem their brokenness, bind up their wounds, love them with an everlasting love, and carry them like the faithful, loving Shepherd He is.

Unfortunately, we hear things like . . . why would a loving God allow suffering at all? This brings His goodness, His character, and His faithfulness into question. This is exactly what the enemy wants us to do. Instead of asking why, seeking to understand and comprehend the mind of God, praise Him for who you know Him to be. Again, this cannot be done outside of an intimate relationship with Him. If you do not yet know of His true character, His faithfulness, and how deep His love runs for you and if you do not yet know that He can be trusted completely, then what will you praise Him for? People? Places? Things? All of this is temporal and fleeting. What if He allows these things to be stripped from you? Your gratitude must run deeper. It is not as if you cannot be grateful for these things. You should be, and expressing our thankfulness is fitting, but that cannot be the focus. Gratitude for who He is should always be our focus.

It may be that you are feeling so dejected, you can barely speak or even think. Be assured, the Holy Spirit will speak for you in groanings too deep for words (see Romans 8:26), so sit quietly in His presence, acknowledging Him. Something else I have enjoyed in my relationship with Him is praise through song. Maybe you do not have words of praise and maybe trying to sit still and quiet before the LORD is a lost cause because your mind is racing. Praise Him through song. We know from scripture that when David played the harp, the evil, tormenting spirit departed from Saul. We do need to be careful and vigilantly discerning when it comes to which music we choose, however. Perhaps you could choose music that has been put to the words of scripture, which is also a great way to memorize God's Word.

I just recently went through a time of fasting and prayer (a time of humbling), in which the LORD revealed many things to me, namely deceptions and hidden sins. One of those revelations was in regard to the "worship" music to which I had been listening. Unfortunately, much of today's modern "Christian" music is flirting with, and in some cases entrenched in, Eastern mystic religion/the occult (aka worship of Lucifer). Now, I know that is a hard statement to hear, but I feel a burden to help bring this to light. No one is immune to this deception. I love the LORD so very much, I love the Word of God so very much, and I have sought to live my life set apart by rejecting and separating from *many* ungodly things in our everyday lives. Yet, I was sucked into this dangerous culture which is nothing short of demonic.

The reason it is so difficult to spot is because it is cloaked in Christian language. This music is specifically designed to seduce our spiritual and physical senses. It can produce a hypnotic effect and, in some cases, draw us into worship of something that is not God Almighty of the Bible. It is appealing to our carnal desire for sensuality, euphoria, and that which makes us feel good. This music is composed in such a way that it creates an emotional experience which is being called evidence of God's presence and Holy Spirit. And many will follow their sensuality, and because of them the way of truth will be blasphemed (II Peter 2:2). For certain people have crept in unnoticed who long ago were designated for this condemnation, ungodly people, who pervert the grace of our God into sensuality and deny our only Master and Lord, Jesus Christ (Jude 1:4).

After mourning and repenting of this completely unintentional sin, a stronghold lifted that I did not even know was there. The more of the world we cut out of our lives, the more sensitive we become to the Spirit of God. We are then able to hear and heed His voice better as we grow closer to Him. Like Paul, indeed, I count everything as loss because of the surpassing worth of knowing Christ Jesus my

Lord. For His sake I have suffered the loss of all things and count them as rubbish, in order that I may gain Christ (Philippians 3:8).

Beware of the Christian music industry and be watchful. I am not going to name a bunch of names and give a lot of details because the truth is readily available for those who really want it. I merely want to sound the alarm and alert you that something is very wrong in the Contemporary Christian Music industry. Very wrong. Apart from the vast repertoire of shallow, me-centered lyrics and vain repetition, there are many who have been flirting with darkness and using occult symbolism on their albums; some whose performances are completely rooted in the occult; many who are speaking new age, prosperity, and universalist heresies; and many who are associating themselves with heretical preachers/false teachers. It is worship for sure, but it is not worship of God Almighty. Trust me, I understand if this is difficult to hear. It was *very* difficult for me, but please bear with me. I am going to provide a couple of examples, but this *by no means* will be the extent of it.

A Bethel worship leader by the name of Amanda Lindsey Cook, who also travels with Hillsong, was nominated for a Dove award (Christian music award); yet, she is openly practicing Islamic Mysticism on stage. She posted a tweet quoting somebody named Rumi, which said, "You're water. We're the millstone. You're wind. We're dust blown up into shapes. You're Spirit. We're the opening and closing of our hands. You're the clarity. We're the language that tries to say it. You're joy. We're all the different kinds of laughing." According to Wikipedia, Rumi is a 13th century Persian, Islamic scholar, theologian, and Sufi mystic (mystic sect of Islam). Sufi dancing is common in Turkey and the Islamic world. They spin around and chant

Allah. There is video of Amanda on stage saying, "I feel like the lord is telling us we need to spin around," and she draws the congregation into her Sufi whirling (the symbolic imitation of planets orbiting the sun). The pastor then gets up and talks about spinning and the universe, and he says, "So what looks like chaos is actually what God put in place as order." This is not worship of God Almighty of the Bible.

Bethel Church members have taken pictures of themselves "grave soaking" atop deceased preachers' graves in an attempt to "soak up" the deceased's "anointing." This is obviously from the occult.

Kirk Franklin is rapping garbage such as, "The lion and the lamb will bow down to the goat." Are you kidding me? He is a deceitful Luciferian pretending to be a Christian, and he is not the only one.

Then, there is the issue of the Kundalini spirit. This comes from Hinduism and originated around the eighth century. Kundalini yoga was then brought over to North America in 1969. It is believed that kundalini energy rests *like a coiled serpent* at the base of the spine. As this energy then flows upward through the seven chakras (energy centers), it leads to an expanded state of consciousness known as a kundalini awakening. An awakening can evoke a strong feeling of euphoria, shaking/jerking/convulsing, psychic/"prophetic" visions, repeating mantras, profound transformation of consciousness/spirituality, long emotional upheavals, and a trance-like state or loss of consciousness. It seems that if we were to replace the word Kundalini spirit with the word Holy Spirit, the extreme charismatic movements are explained.

What we can see demonstrated by Hillsong, Bethel, and others who perform this music on stage is that of a Kundalini awakening (the demonic Eastern Mystic concept of a force moving through you which causes involuntary reactions). You can see the snake-like movements as they worship. You can see the emotional frenzy and the euphoria, both on stage and in the crowd, and you can recognize the repetitive chants and mantras once you realize what this is really all about. In addition to being psychologically proven to create pleasure for the listener, chanting and verbal repetition in singing has been noted to open one's mind to suggestion and open the spirit to influence. We have become lovers of pleasure more than lovers of God, having an appearance of godliness but denying its power (II Timothy 3:4-5).

I no longer listen to Hillsong, Bethel, Jesus Culture, Elevation, Maverick City, Jesus Image, and many others. They are not trying to lift up Christ; they are trying to lift up experience, and those of us who are true Bible-believing Christians have no business participating in any of this. Beloved, do not believe every spirit, but test the spirits to see whether they are from God, for many false prophets have gone out into the world (I John 4:1). Now the Spirit speaketh expressly, that in the latter times some shall depart from the faith, giving heed to seducing spirits, and doctrines of devils (I Timothy 4:1, KJV). If you think you can detach the actions of those who make the music from the music itself, remember this: A corrupt tree cannot bring forth good fruit (see Luke 6:43b, KJV).

These spirits are seducing us into a euphoric type of worship through the music, which appeals to our carnal desire for sensuality and pleasure. I was deceived by this, and many are being deceived by this. It feels like a heightened spiritual experience with God. He knew my heart as I took part in this, and I do believe that there were times He used this evil for good in my life. However, in His grace, He showed me the truth, which then placed a responsibility upon me to turn away from it because it is evil. This music is a part of a feelings-based religion where we no longer rely on God's Word but on our feelings, experience, and emotions. Dangerous! We are easily deceived by our emotions. This is nothing more than a carnal desire for sensuality. To think that something which makes us feel good cannot possibly be bad is, of course, a dark lie.

You may be thinking that these statements are ludicrous because the lyrics are singing about devotion to Jesus Christ. We must be careful with this logic. In addition to the fact that music is not neutral, there is another "Jesus" being preached, and it has been going on for centuries. But I am afraid that as the serpent deceived Eve by his cunning, your thoughts will be led astray from a sincere and pure devotion to Christ. For if someone comes and proclaims *another Jesus* than the one we proclaimed, or if you receive *a different spirit* from the one you received, or if you accept *a different gospel* from the one you accepted, you put up with it readily enough (I Corinthians 11:3-4, italics added). There is another "Jesus" being proclaimed, which I will speak on further in Chapter Six. I strongly urge you to seek God's guidance and beg Him for discernment because there are many wolves in sheep's clothing singing about "Jesus." It is written, "Take away from me the noise of your songs; to the melody of your harps I will not listen" (Amos 5:23).

Up until recently, I had never seen this music performed. I had only listened to it on the radio or sang it in church or what have you, and I am sure many of you are in the same boat. Aside from the snake-like movements, there are other hand gestures and motions made that have eerily striking similarities with that of a witch casting a spell or trying to harness and control "energy." Here's a super creepy side note. Prior to ever seeing any of these performances, these very same hand gestures and motions came out of me. The few times this happened, I thought, huh, that was kind of weird. Once I began to learn the truth, I was mortified.

It broke my heart to realize my unfaithfulness to God as I participated in this "worship," unaware of the true intended recipient. Our enemy is so very clever. I thank God that where sin abounds, grace abounds the more, and praise be to God Almighty that He remains faithful to us even in our unfaithfulness. I was appalled to learn of all this and broken over my sin against Him but also equally in awe over His Amazing Grace and patience for a wretched sinner like me. I have shared with you some extreme examples, of which there are many more. Disturbingly, there are also many subtle ways in which this music is leading people astray and far away from the LORD. Please be careful and be on guard.

God will bless you with His presence when you seek to praise Him in spite of your circumstances. We were created with the desire to feel good and be happy, so naturally no one enjoys suffering, but it does not mean that God is not loving, faithful, good, and just. He is always all of these things and more. Also, it is not as if He enjoys watching us suffer; nothing could be further from the truth. In fact, when one of His beloved children is in the midst of suffering, He is near to them. He heals the brokenhearted and binds up their wounds (Psalm 147:3). The LORD is near to all who call on Him, to all who call on Him in truth (Psalm 145:18). Jesus Christ was weeping at the tomb of Lazarus, I believe, to show us that just as God calls us to weep with those who weep, in a sense, He weeps with us.

We walk by faith and not by sight, but of this you can be sure: If you are His child, He has got your back, and He always will. He will never fail you, and He will never let you down. If you feel He has failed you or let you down in some way, take heart, He would never ever do that. He may be trying to teach you something or He may be drawing you nearer to Himself. Whatever His reasons, He has your best interest and His higher purposes in mind. Do not let the enemy tell you that your God is not faithful to you. Our God is faithful even though we are not! He is committed to you. How immeasurable is the depth and height and width and length of His great love for us!

When I turned my back on God, He was faithful. Before I realized who He is to me, He was faithful. Before I realized who I was to Him, He was faithful. As we stepped out in faith over and over again, He was faithful. When I do not know where to go or what to do, He is faithful. When I do not know when to speak up and when to be silent, He is faithful. When I am in over my head and feel like I am drowning, He is faithful. As we pray for others, He is faithful. He remains faithful regardless of our faithfulness (or lack thereof). If we are faithless, He remains faithful (II Timothy 2:13). That is definitely cause for praise even, and especially, through the storms and trials of life.

When it seems so dark we cannot see our own hand in front of our face, we can take confidence in Him who remains faithful to us in every conceivable way. The dark is as light to Him. He sees it all, and He will see us through it all. As we face various trials, we also face a choice. Will we grumble and complain, perhaps even shaking a fist at God, or will we praise Him, knowing and believing He will work it out for good even though His good purposes and intentions may not be immediately perceived?

One day, my daughter began to reminisce about a small New Testament Bible she used to have and how she wanted another one. My son chimed in saying, "I want one too!" I stopped walking and came around to the front of the stroller. Bending down, I said, "You know, we ought to pray and ask God to provide a small Bible for each of you," and we did just that.

Several weeks later, through a series of events, we missed our bus by a few minutes. With an hour-long wait ahead of us, I could have easily grumbled and, in fact, was tempted to do so. However, I resolved that God is in control, and it happened, so let us make the best of it. I realized there was a park nearby where we could easily kill time as we waited on the next bus. We headed that direction. As we stood at the stoplight waiting to cross the street, I looked over, and I could not believe my eyes. There sat a brand new mini New Testament Bible still in the wrapper. My heart leapt as I knew it was the answer to our prayer. I started to think, too bad there is not another one, but I should have known better because in that instant, I turned my head to see an identical mini Bible lying on the bench. Extraordinary! His presence was overwhelming, and my children and I praised and glorified God. I am so grateful when they get to taste and see that the LORD is good!

I could have been irritated and even angry about the reasons I missed that bus, but by the grace of God, I prayerfully accepted the circumstance, continuing in thankfulness within. Little did I know at the time, a glimpse of God's glory, an answer to prayer, and the joy of His felt presence lay just up ahead. I realize this was more of an inconvenience than a trial, but I was faced with the choice, nonetheless; and it is a perfect example of God's faithfulness at work *for* me when the circumstances appear to be *against* me. It can be just as easily applied to the much larger trials we face in life, whether that be great loss, sickness, or facing uncertainty in the upheaval of things. We can be sure He is at work for us and not against us (those who love Him).

With all this in mind, I implore you, relinquish worrying through your storm and begin to praise Him through it. This starts with cultivating a deep and intimate relationship with Him during the calm. Consequently, when the catastrophic storm arises, you know whom you have believed, and you can stand on the promises of the Word of God, praising Him all the way, for great is His faithfulness.

- I have said these things to you that in me you may have peace. In the world, you will have tribulation. But take heart; I have overcome the world (John 16:33).
- The crucible is for silver, and the furnace is for gold, and a man is tested by his praise (Proverbs 27:21).
- I will bless the LORD at all times. His praise shall continually be in my mouth (Psalm 34:1).
- In the day of prosperity, be joyful, and in the day of adversity, consider: God has made the one as well as the other (Ecclesiastes 7:14).

CHAPTER FIVE

The Presence of the LORD – Seek Him First

You have said, seek my face.
My heart says to you, your face LORD do I seek.
Psalm 27:8

I AM GOING TO go out on a limb here and say, the most important thing we will ever do (once we belong to the kingdom of God) is seek the face (presence) of the LORD, especially through His Word. He promises that if we seek, we will find, so we are left with no excuse. Spending intimate time with Him and actively acknowledging His presence is, without a doubt, the way our relationship moves out of the shallow and into the deep. You cannot cultivate a marriage, friendship, or any kind of relationship apart from spending quality time together. It is no different in our marriage/friendship/relationship with God through Christ.

As stated in I Chronicles 10:11, we must seek the LORD *continually*. There is no joy that comes close to comparing with the fullness of joy found in the presence of the LORD. Do not misunderstand me. His presence is with us always. He will never leave us nor forsake us, so I do not mean to convey to you that His presence comes and goes; it does not. His Holy Spirit dwells inside of us who believe, which is a powerful truth too often taken for granted. He is Immanuel, the "with us God." The question is, are we with Him? Many of us have become so utterly distracted by the busyness of life that we have neglected to acknowledge Him and spend intimate time with Him on a frequent and consistent basis. In doing so, we are made vulnerable to attack, we are unable to stand, and we are overcome by anxious thoughts and fears. True surrender goes hand in hand with real relationship, and both have been traded in for religious activity. Folks, there is a better way.

The story of Martha and Mary found in Luke 10 is a good example. My natural tendency is to be busy like Martha, but the LORD has been showing me how to be still like Mary. For anyone possibly unfamiliar with this story, it goes like this: A woman named Martha welcomed Him (Jesus Christ) into her house. Now, she had a sister named Mary who sat at the Lord's feet and listened to His teaching, but Martha was distracted with much serving. She said, "Lord, do you not care that my sister has left me to serve alone? Tell her to help me," but the Lord answered her, "Martha, Martha, you are anxious and troubled about many things, but only one thing is necessary. Mary has chosen the good portion, which will not be taken away from her." *Only one thing is necessary.*

That is not to say there is not a time to go out into the world and do. The scriptures tell us that God has prepared good works in which we ought to walk. Sadly, however, many are distracted by the doing and have lost touch with the one necessary thing, sitting humbly in the presence of our Lord and Savior, Jesus Christ. Rest in His presence is a beautiful gift He longs to give each one of us. When my flesh or another voice tells me, you need to _____ (fill in the blank), but I know God is encouraging me to spend time with Him, there is tremendous reward in responding accordingly. He is our very great reward. In addition, the things that do need to get done are somehow done more efficiently and effectively. Incredibly, it sometimes seems as if He even slows down time itself. He wants to be first, He deserves to be first, and you will find true joy when you make Him first.

Shortly after being separated from my children, I began to seek the presence of the LORD, but it was not a straight climb. I climbed and fell many times over several years as I still desired to retain some "control" and lacked complete surrender. I also held onto a lot of pride, so I remained deceived regarding my own strength and ability, which apart from Christ does not exist. In essence, it remained sort of a half-hearted seeking, but He blessed me in those moments, none-theless. Why? Because we serve a faithful God who remains faithful. Thus says the LORD: The people who survived the sword found grace in the wilderness; when Israel sought for rest, the LORD appeared to me from far away. I have loved you with an everlasting love; there-fore, I have continued my faithfulness to you (Jeremiah 31:2-3). The KJV reads, therefore, with lovingkindness I have drawn thee. I don't know about you, but that speaks volumes to my heart.

Finally, in July 2019, I was utterly at my wit's end. Mine and my children's lives were hanging in the balance, I was completely sepa-rated from my other children, and I knew my iniquities had gone way over my head. Threats of murder were being hurled at me, demonic things were happening all around me, and I waved my white flag and threw myself upon the mercy of God. I spent that entire night in worship of and in the presence of the LORD. It was unlike anything I had ever known. There is none like Him. No wonder it says, what no eye has seen nor ear has heard nor the heart of man imagined what God has prepared for those who love Him. I cannot adequately describe the awe or the peace that floods my being when I am acknowledging His presence, and these are but small glimpses (even a shadow) of the glory that will be revealed. Wow! I know many of you know exactly what I am talking about. Still, others may not. I encourage you – Seek Him with all your heart, soul, and mind. You will not be disappointed. You will be blown away.

This night was a catalyst for many more intimate moments with my Lord and Savior, for which I am so grateful. Believe it or not, being unable to drive has turned out to be an enormous blessing. How wonderful the fellowship with God has been on many a long walk. There is nothing like enjoying intimate fellowship with God; there is no one like Him. I began to know and recognize that still, small voice. My sheep hear my voice; I know them, and they follow me (John 10:27). It was a voice I had heard as a child and a voice which attempted to speak to me all throughout my life, but my sin and indifference had drowned it out. I had become dull of hearing and my heart was hard. Now, however, in a truly surrendered state, my ears were opened, and the eyes of my heart enlightened to know and recognize my Shepherd's voice once more, which is a joy and a delight. So, I have found that seeking the LORD while walking has been extremely beneficial to our relationship, and I would highly recommend it.

You can seek God's presence at anytime, anywhere, and no matter what you may be doing. This goes hand in hand with our call to pray without ceasing. We can continually acknowledge God and seek

Him through our inner self in every moment of the day. There are times in which this may require more discipline and effort and other times, such as in the midst of suffering, where this will be much easier to attain. Whether it is easy or difficult and whether we are in the midst of suffering or in the midst of the mundane and routine aspects of our lives, we should be striving to acknowledge God's presence in every moment.

My comfort in my affliction is that His promise gives me life (Psalm 119:50). His promise gives me eternal life, yes, but also abundant life now. Abundant life, in my opinion, is all about the peace and the joy that comes with acknowledging the presence of God. We had to leave our home with nothing to avoid being murdered; there was not one soul on earth that I could call; I did not know where we were going to go; and I was not even sure we would make it through the night; but His presence and the intimate fellowship we shared was so unimaginably wonderful, it made all of those things seem insignificant. I realized in every fiber of my being that I am in a relationship with my God, and He is ALL that I need. His promise gives me life, both now and forever.

It is vital that we seek Him through the reading of His Word. The scriptures have taught me of the true nature and character of God, and it is a powerful way in which He speaks to me many times daily. He guides, convicts, and comforts me through His Word. He does so much with His Word. Please do not take it for granted. It is extremely important.

It is true there are other ways to connect with the LORD, such as prayer and worship. I have spoken of intimacy with Him prior to knowing His Word at all. Sure, I had done some Bible studies and maybe sort of heard something in church, but I did not know it. I did not read it. I took it for granted. Yes, He met me with open arms while I was still a long way off, but I was not going to stay there, ignorant of His Word. No. Right off the bat, He was putting strong urges in my spirit to read it as much and as often as I had time to do so.

It really does come alive, and I am continually in awe of God's ways. The way that He orchestrates so perfectly His Word and the way He weaves it throughout my life is mind blowing. The more involved I am with the scriptures, the more amazement and awe to follow. It is always relevant to what I am currently dealing with or meditating on, and the same scriptures will show up in multiple places. He weaves it throughout my devotionals, my handwritten index cards, books I read, what I hear in church or Bible study, and what happens to come up in just normal conversation. There is no explanation for it beyond the fact that God's sovereignty is so much more powerful than we could ever comprehend. When I know that He has just spoken to me through what I just read in the Bible, again, I am flooded with the sense of His presence. This always puts a big smile on my face because I am astonished at the way in which He does that every day. It blows my mind, and I love that about Him.

Another way we can seek His presence is through worship in song. How many beautiful and intimate moments I have shared with God as I praise Him with singing. How many beautiful moments we have had as a family worshiping our God through song. It so fills me with the beauty of His presence, and I am always in awe. Often on our walks, a good portion of our time spent with Him has been in praising Him through song, and the LORD truly inhabits the praises of His people, without a doubt. So, worship through singing is a beautiful way to connect to Him and through which to seek His presence.

The presence of God has navigated us through unknown lands full of unknown people time and time again. Throughout this wilderness journey, the joy of His presence has flooded my being often as He has reiterated His power and His love for me in extremely tangible ways. I was "alone" in these unknown lands, yet not alone at all. My God was watching over us and providing for us in every possible way, and His intimate presence has been my comfort through it all. For the LORD God takes me by the hand and says to me, fear not! I am the one who helps you (Isaiah 41:13). Glory be to God. He loves all of His children with an intense, everlasting love, and nothing happens to us that does not go through Him first. Our times are in his hand.

There was a point in the fall of 2021 that I began to notice a sense of dryness in my relationship with Him. I was still talking to Him, and I was still in His Word, but it seemed that something was missing. I just could not put my finger on it. He even went so far as to say to me, I know you are enduring patiently and bearing up for my name's sake and you have not grown weary, but I have this against you, that you have abandoned the love you had at the first. Remember, therefore, from where you have fallen and repent, doing the works you did at the first (from Revelation 2).

I knew the last few weeks felt dry, but why? After a few weeks of oddity I did not understand, I would then find myself sitting in a church service, in which the pastor would speak about seeking God's presence. There it was – The missing piece. Even though I had continued in the reading of His Word and prayer, I had neglected the pursuit of intimacy with Him. Not only that, but I had been seeking outside of His will what I was going to do to bring in an income. I had stopped seeking Him and His righteousness first. Gratefully, He put a stop to my wandering.

The pastor went on to talk about how when we seek God's presence, God moves. He said, stop focusing on the employment you are seeking, or the relationship that needs fixing, or the bills you can't pay, and seek God. He will bring you that opportunity, that repair, and that provision in His time (I am paraphrasing). This sermon cut straight to my heart. God had revealed where I had gone wrong, how I had left my first love. My response, by God's grace, was repentance through tears and lifted hands in worship of God. I asked Him to forgive me, and He renewed my desire to keep Him first. This was the first time I had words to describe what I had been doing the last couple of years – Seeking His presence. I never would have called it that prior to this; I did not know what to call it other than amazing.

Interestingly, I walked out of that service wherein I put God back where He belonged and humbled myself by casting all my cares upon Him, and I was approached by a woman/friend who offered me a possible job watching her dog. Seek ye first the kingdom of God and His righteousness, and all these things will be added unto you. Transportation issues would hinder bringing this to fruition, but it proved the pastor's words true.

Over and over, God had proven to me that I do not need to worry about what I will eat, drink, or wear. However, I had allowed the thoughts of others as well as my own sense of responsibility to override seeking Him first and trusting Him for everything else. You need not worry about the possibility of overlooking something He wants you to do. If you need to act, the LORD will urge you to act. First, we would do well to seek Him with all our heart and soul. He is all-powerful to guide you, but first, make Him first. Seek His presence continually. Hebrews 11:6 says, and without faith, it is impossible to please Him for whoever would draw near to God must believe that He exists and that *He rewards those who seek Him* (italics added). The KJV says, He is a rewarder of them that diligently seek Him. If you seek Him (diligently), He will be found by you. We see that promise time and again in the scriptures. Take Him up on it!

As mentioned, I was ignorant of the Bible for most of my life, but there was one scripture of which I was very familiar, Jeremiah 29:11. The LORD spoke to me in my early 20s saying, I know the plans I have for you, and I would realize this was a verse in the Bible as it increased in popularity and became a common scripture to put up on your wall. What I would come to know, as I actually read the Bible, were verses 12 and 13. These are powerful verses which spoke to my heart and described my new relationship with the LORD. In its entirety, it goes like this: For I know the plans I have for you, declares the LORD, plans for welfare (or peace) and not for evil, to give you a future and a hope. Then you will call upon me and come and pray to me, and I will hear you. You will seek me and find me. When you seek me with all your heart, I will be found by you, declares the LORD. What a beautiful truth. Because of the precious blood of Jesus Christ, we have 24/7 access to the presence of the King, and we are not only accepted into His presence but rewarded for seeking Him out, every time.

Please allow me to warn you, however, that there is a counterfeit "presence" at work in the world of Christianity today. There are many false teachers leading people astray using a counterfeit "presence of

God," often referred to as the "presence of the Holy Spirit." It is not God or His Spirit; it is something else entirely. Seeking and enjoying the presence of God is biblical, and it is a beautiful thing. We see this in Psalm repeatedly. Just remember: Everything that God does, the enemy tries to imitate in a twisted manner. Oftentimes, when we hear about the presence of God or the presence of the Holy Spirit in these last days, it is tied to a sensual, feelings-based mystery religion which focuses on emotional experience. Please be careful and be on guard.

I did not want to put too much emphasis on the next aspect I want to speak on because God, himself, is our very great reward, but I do not want to overlook the phenomenal provision given us by Him either.

The earth is the LORD's and the fullness thereof, and He appropriates His resources as He deems fit. This is what He kept bringing to mind as He called me into His work and away from working for an income. To be clear, He did not call me away from work. We are all called to work for the glory of God. He has specific tasks and jobs for us all, and we ought not be slothful. However, He definitely took me out of mainstream employment for several seasons.

For three years, I have had no income, none. This includes no food stamps or assistance as this was not the LORD's will for me. Nevertheless, my children and I have never lacked or wanted for anything. We have not only survived, we have thrived. He has proven He has an endless number of ways in which He comes through for us when we have needed something.

We have never lacked food, clothing, or shelter. We have never lacked diapers, wipes, or baby formula. We have never lacked a functional stroller, which gets us to where we need to go. For the most part, we have always had fruits, vegetables, and good proteins on hand. On the rare occasion we have needed money, the LORD provides that as well. I have had so many complete strangers come up to me and say, "May I give you some money?" We do not look needy. It was purely and simply the LORD moving hearts to fill a need. I have never seen the righteous abandoned or their children begging for bread (Psalm 37:25). We never have. Those who seek the LORD lack no good thing (Psalm 34:10). We never have. We have always been able to clean our clothes and our bodies. Cleanliness is important to me, and God, in His kindness, provides.

For three months, no extras were provided. I had two of the most hideous outfits I have ever owned and wore no make-up. I simply had the bare necessities, and I was content. It is not that He did not want me to have things, but He did not want things to have me, and I am thankful for that.

I once thought it would be nice to have a black hoodie with thumb holes. That night I found one hanging on my doorknob. More than once, I wanted a soft blanket for my children or for myself, and more than once I was given one. My water bottle broke, and the next day, a woman, who did not know that, handed me a better one. I wanted a prayer journal with scripture on the pages in which to write, and an hour later, someone offered me a journal with scripture printed on the pages. It had been collecting dust on her shelf for the past three years. My children needed warm winter hats, and I found some on the ground that were in perfect condition, one pink and one gray. After I washed them, they were like new. I wanted another notebook, and I found one in a donated box near a clothes bin. I wanted a coffee mug, and I found one two days later in a similar box. I wanted a bookmark for the kids' devotional, and the next day someone handed me one with one of our memorized verses on it, Deuteronomy 31:6. Someone gave us a bunch of shorts one summer, and I thought, if I just had a bunch of white T-shirts, we would be set. That evening we went for a walk, and we came across a bag someone had tossed to the side of the road. Clothes had been spilled out of it, and there lay nineteen white T-shirts, exactly their size, white like new, no stains. I wanted an electric toothbrush for my children, and He provided. We needed schoolbooks and supplies, He provided. We needed beginner's reading material, and a woman from church gave me some unexpectedly. We needed addition flashcards, and our neighbor, who did not know that, handed me some. My children wanted tiny Bibles, He provided.

I could go on and on and on, filling many pages (probably an entire book) recounting the plethora of things the LORD has provided through uncanny and sometimes mysterious ways. And God is able to make all grace abound to you, so that having all sufficiency in all things at all times, you may abound in every good work (II Corinthians 9:8). It reminds me of Luke 22:35. And He said to them, "When I sent you out with no moneybag or knapsack or sandals, did you lack anything?" They said, "Nothing." With a smile on my face, I think, what is man that you are mindful of him? It is inconceivable!

Seek first the kingdom of God and His righteousness, and all these things will be added unto you. Whatever "these things" are for you, He has got your back. You can trust Him to take care of you in whatever way is necessary for your calling, but you must devote time to rest in His presence; you must devote time to His Word; and you must seek Him first, frequently, and before everything and everyone else.

- You make known to me the path of life; in your presence, there is fullness of joy; at your right hand are pleasures forevermore (Psalm 16:11).
- For it is time to seek the LORD that He may come and rain righteousness upon you (Hosea 10:12).
- Seek the LORD while He may be found. Call upon Him while He is near (Isaiah 55:6).
- Seek the LORD and His strength. Seek His presence continually (Psalm 105:4).

CHAPTER SIX

The Land of Idolatry

Little children, keep yourselves from idols!
I John 5:21

AS WE DIVE INTO this next chapter, which may at times feel challenging, I would like to take a moment to explain its true purpose. As I scratch the surface on the many different forms of idolatry prevalent in our world today, it is not meant to be read as a list of rules. It is not a checklist and is by no means a complete list. It is only the tip of the iceberg.

It is intended to shed light on some of the many ways we have turned our backs on God and His Word as we have become complacent in our sin and idolatry. At its very core, it is a call to repent and return to the LORD with our whole heart, mind, and soul in faithfulness to Him because we love Him. Words like repent and obey have become taboo in the name of grace, and this should not be the case at all. Separating faithful obedience from the Christian walk in the name of grace has led to intense corruption. It is time for us to break free from this corruption in the name of faithfulness.

So, what is an idol? It is anyone or anything we exalt into the position that belongs to God alone. It is the first commandment that we have no other gods besides the One True Living God (YHWH Elohim), none. Yet, many of us are living in bondage to idolatry.

God has said, you shall be holy (set apart) to me for I, the LORD, am holy and have separated you from the peoples that you should be mine (Leviticus 20:26). Yet, many of us are daily taking part in abomination, either indifferent to or ignorant of the fact that it is detestable in His sight. God is the same yesterday, today, and forever, and idolatry kindles the anger of the LORD. If you transgress the covenant of the LORD your God, which He commanded you, and go and serve other gods and bow down to them, then the anger of the LORD will be kindled against you (Joshua 23:16).

Our idolatry kindles His anger and rightly so; it is betrayal and adultery. He alone deserves all of our worship, praise, and adoration. When we give His glory to another person, an object, or to an idea it is a great insult to Him because there is none like Him.

Paul says, do not be conformed to this world but be transformed by the renewal of your mind, that by testing you may discern what is the will of God, what is good, acceptable, and perfect (Romans 12:2). James goes so far as to say, you adulterous people! Do you not know that friendship with the world is enmity with God? Therefore, whoever wishes to be a friend of the world makes himself an enemy of God (James 4:4). Clearly, we are not to conform to the world around us. Yet, in many cases, you often cannot readily perceive a distinction between the two groups of people (those who believe and follow Christ and those who reject Him). Our lives should look much different from theirs, but I am afraid we have given in to the idolatry of the nations around us and have accepted it as a normal part of our lives.

Why are we so blind to the will of God when, according to scripture, we are given the ability to discern His perfect and acceptable will? Wherefore be ye not unwise (ESV, foolish), but understanding what the will of the LORD is (Ephesians 5:17, KJV). I submit it is because we are not aiming to please God as we ought. Instead, we have become fixated upon pleasing ourselves (self-worship). We have become fixated upon our comfort, our pleasure, our convenience, and our will at the cost of freedom and obedience to the LORD's commands and His perfect desire and will for our lives. Too easily, we shrug off God's direction when it comes into conflict with our flesh. For at one time you were darkness, but now you are light in the LORD. Walk as children of light for the fruit of light is found in all that is good and right and true and try to discern what is pleasing to the LORD (Ephesians 5:8-10).

This cannot be done outside of an intimate relationship with Him. Have you ever noticed the closer and more intimate you become with another person, the more your likes and dislikes seem to line up? That is how it works in our relationship with our God as well. The more deeply we fall in love with Him, the more we will desire to love what He loves and abhor what He abhors (detests).

Luke 16:15 says, what is exalted among men is an abomination in the sight of God. This is a litmus test that has never failed me. In my journey to seek and discover what is fully pleasing to God and what is not, I have often used this scripture to ask the question, is it widely accepted among the masses? Is it exalted among men? If so, according to scripture, it is abomination in the sight of God.

As you start to seek out these truths, you will probably be surprised at some of the things you find. I know I have been. Enter by the narrow gate for the gate is wide and the way is easy that leads to destruction, and those who enter by it are many. For the gate is narrow and the way is hard that leads to life, and those who find it are few (Matthew 7:13-14). First, this verse is speaking of Jesus being the only Way, the narrow gate to life, but secondly, I see an application toward that which I am speaking.

It is widely accepted to exalt ourselves, our spouse, our children, possessions, power, career, money, drugs and alcohol in some circles; comfort, pleasure, entertainment, sports, celebrities, food, sex, appearance, fashion, our bodies, our ego, our pride, and even religious activity which we use to feed our egos through "good" deeds. Yet, abundant life is not found in the exaltation of any of these things. In fact, it only leads to destruction. True life is found in Christ alone.

We were created by God Almighty to worship, so the question is not *if* we will worship, the question is *who* or *what* will we worship. How about you? Are you worshiping the creature/created things or are you worshiping the Creator? For although they knew God, they did not honor Him as God or give thanks to Him, but they became futile in their thinking, and their foolish hearts were darkened. Claiming to be wise, they became fools and exchanged the glory of the immortal God for images resembling mortal man and birds and animals and creeping things. Therefore, God gave them up in the lusts of their hearts to impurity, to the dishonoring of their bodies among themselves because they exchanged the truth about God for a lie and worshiped and served the creature rather than the Creator (Romans 1:21-25). I have been so guilty of this. This scripture shot straight to my heart when I first read it.

Idolatry is a terrible tragedy which has infiltrated the lives of God's children everywhere. The deceitfulness of sin and idolatry has hardened hearts; the Spirit and voice of God have been quenched; and we are living just as they did in the times of the Judges as everyone does what seems right in their own eyes. The LORD looks down from Heaven on the children of man to see if there are any who understand, who seek after God. They have all turned aside; together, they have become corrupt. There is none who does good, not even one (Psalm 14:2-3). There is no fear of God before their eyes (Romans 3:18).

The fear of the LORD is hatred of evil (Proverbs 8:13a). Instead of hating evil and turning from it, many are relishing and delighting in it. I have in many ways. How horrifying. How do you think that makes God feel? Loved? Cherished? I think not. Just look at the TV programs and movies that have been allowed into our homes. This so-called entertainment, that is many times anti-God, anti-creation, and anti-Bible truth, often promotes crude joking, sex, drugs, and violence, not to mention wizards and witchcraft. Whether this is blatant or subliminal, whether this is live persons or cartoons, it is detestable, and this is only one example of the ways in which we take delight in evil abomination. These have chosen their own ways, and their soul delights in their abominations; I also will choose harsh treatment for them and bring their fears upon them because when I called, no one answered. When I spoke, they did not listen, but they did what was evil in my eyes and chose that in which I did not delight. Hear the Word of the LORD, you who tremble at His Word (Isaiah 66:3-5).

Some idolatry is painfully obvious; some is much more subtle. There was a time when someone gave me a really nice, really comfortable Nike hoodie. However, as soon as I put it on, I heard that still, small voice say, "Do not wear that. Take it off." I had a decision to make. Would I choose comfort and style over obedience to my God? By the grace of God, no, I would obey. He impressed upon my spirit that this particular brand was named after an idol. That impression would turn out to be truth. It is named after an ancient Greek so-called goddess, and the emblem is supposed to be one of her wings. We are not even supposed to have the name of any false god upon our lips, much less wear it as decoration upon our clothes. Joshua 23:7 says, you may not mix with these nations remaining among you or make mention of the names of their gods . . . vs. 11, be very careful, therefore, to love the LORD your God. In Exodus 23:13, it says, pay attention to all that I have said to you and make no mention of the names of other gods nor let it be heard on your lips!

At another time, I began to take notice of the rise in the popularity of mermaids. I thought to myself, this is really becoming exalted among men; you see the obsession everywhere. Could this be an abomination? I inquired of the LORD. He answered me by way of a book I checked out from the library about ancient Babylon. In this book, He showed me how, indeed, there was a false god of Babylon, which was supposedly part fish.

There is a deep, dark deception thriving in our world today. The enemy's cunning tactics are much more nefarious than many people realize, and it is the truth which sets us free. It is not as if Nike is the only brand flaunting idolatry or as if mermaids are the only symbols of idolatry. There are literally thousands more; these are merely examples. Now, therefore, fear the LORD and serve Him in sincerity and in faithfulness. Put away the gods that your fathers served . . . and serve the LORD (Joshua 24:14).

Consumerism/materialism has run rampant, has it not? Advertising and store shelves are specifically designed to cause us to covet, breeding discontent and always a desire for more. It is abomination in direct contrast with God's will; yet, we have all been guilty of succumbing at some point. I have made it a practice to pray prior to entering and while inside of a store, saying, "LORD, please keep my eyes from whoring." It does work, but only if I ask Him. Otherwise, I am inclined to do what the flesh is inclined to do – Whore after false happiness/false gods by way of things.

Whoring eyes is a concept of which I was first made aware as I finally came to know the Word of God. It is the perfect description for what takes place as we look upon and then exalt an idol. We become unfaithful in our relationship with the LORD as we lust after the things of this world and our own pleasure. This may be a concept hard to swallow, but it is truth. Our God is a jealous God, and it is only a matter of time before calamity falls on an unfaithful wife.

I used to pride myself on my loyalty to people, even to a destructive fault, but where was my loyalty to God, my Savior who rescued me? Once I began to grasp my depravity, it became apparent that God put that loyalty in me for Himself, and here I was giving it away to others and not to Him.

Do you consistently experience friction in your relationships? If so, it is likely that expectations have been placed upon an individual to fill a need or desire deep within, which is meant to be filled by God alone. This can happen within a friendship just as it can within a romantic relationship. Repent and return to the LORD. The ideology that a person or relationship outside of God can complete us or make us whole is false and destructive. It will always end in disaster. Do not put your friends or your spouse above the LORD.

Also, do not put your children above the LORD. Your world should revolve around God only. To put your spouse or your children first is to dethrone the LORD. Of course, love them well, cherish them, and sacrifice for them, but do not ever put them in the position that belongs to the Father and do not do anything for them at the cost of obedience to Him; the end is catastrophic. God will share His glory with no other. If we do not find immense joy in our relationship with Christ alone, apart from everyone and everything else, He will do what He deems necessary to help us understand.

The other person who gets in the way of a right relationship with God is . . . ourselves. We see in II Timothy 3:2 that in the last days there will come times of difficulty, for people will be lovers of self. Boy oh boy, isn't that the truth? In fact, there are some who ardently teach on loving yourself, as if there is any sort of freedom found in this idolatry. I do not suggest that we go around speaking of a hatred of ourselves. Self-loathing is a false humility and also a form of pride (self-worship). That being said, if you have been through significant trauma, as many of us have, you may have a skewed self-image. The answer is not to love yourself more. The answer is to love God more, and He will bring you the healing you need to see yourself more clearly. Shift your focus. Stop trying to *find yourself* and start searching for Jesus Christ with all your heart, mind, and soul.

As believers, we need to be careful as we attempt to console those who may be expressing confusion and sadness about who they are because of trauma they have experienced. When we offer comfort by way of praise and say things such as you are strong, you are a good person, and you are worthy, this comes from the wisdom of the world, which we know is folly to God.

There is a common misconception that people are inherently good. This is a dangerous deception of the enemy. We must agree with God's Word and realize the true human condition for what it is – Depraved and wicked. I do not marvel at the deep, dark evils of this world as though I do not understand how anyone could do such things. I do wonder why more people do not realize the wickedness of which sinners are capable. It may be due to pride and the fact that we do not want to imagine ourselves capable of such things, but truly it is only by the grace of God that we do not spiral into the depths of evil ourselves.

The truth is that apart from Christ, we are weak; our "good" is like filthy, disgusting rags; and we are not worthy. It is only because of Christ's strength and righteousness that we can stand upright. To attribute strength to an individual apart from Christ is false teaching and harmful territory. As we see in the Psalms and in Romans, there is none who does good, not even one. In fact, it is our unworthiness which creates our need for a Savior. If we encourage others to think more highly of themselves than they ought, they likely will not search for the only one who can heal them.

Since the fall of man, we are all born with a seed of rebellion within us that only worsens with time. You say, but I have not killed anyone. Jesus Christ says, "You have heard that it was said to those of old, 'You shall not murder; and whoever murders will be liable to judgment.' But I say to you that everyone who is angry with his brother will be liable to judgment" (Matthew 5:21-22a). We must stop measuring ourselves by one another and measure ourselves by God's Word alone. His Word sets the standard extremely high, even unattainable; you must therefore be perfect as your Heavenly Father is perfect (Matthew 5:48). This is one reason the good news is so good. In His great mercy and His love for us, He has paid our price that we might receive *His* robe of righteousness and *His* perfection.

To attempt to encourage someone who is suffering and filled with low esteem by praising and feeding their ego, suggesting they affirm themselves apart from who they are in Christ, is not helping them. It is actually hurting them. It is to nurture the pride within them. It encourages them to think about themselves more and to become even more self-absorbed. The more we encourage others to focus on themselves, the more their esteem will actually suffer. There is a way that seems right to mankind, but its end is the way to death (Proverbs 14:12).

Instead, we ought to encourage one another in God's truth. Our identity must, first and foremost, be found in Christ alone. Our identity should be grounded in the fact that we are made in the image of God, forgiven, and highly esteemed by God as His beloved children, if this is, indeed, the case. If that covenant has not been made, do not fill them with vain hopes. Apart from Christ, we are sinful, broken, and weak. In contrast to these truths, we have been encouraged by the enemy to think much of ourselves, often. One of his main objectives is to exalt mankind. Why is that? Because if he can keep us blind to who we really are and keep us loving and believing in ourselves, then we will not love or believe God. We will stay blind to our need for a savior and self-affirm ourselves all the way to hell.

I have heard believers say, Jesus said we ought to love our neighbors as ourselves, so that must mean we should love ourselves. I submit this was not at all the point. Instead, we are born loving ourselves. We are naturally inclined to give ourselves what we think we want when we want it no matter the cost. For no one ever hated his own flesh, but nourishes and cherishes it . . . (Ephesians 5:29). Jesus was saying we ought to put the same amount of drive and effort into loving our neighbors. In humility, we ought to consider others more significant than ourselves (Philippians 2:3). To be clear, humility is not thinking less of yourself; it is thinking of yourself less. Our culture is completely self-absorbed. The focus is me, myself, and I. Of course this leads to anxiety and depression because, at its root, it is idolatry (self-worship). We are elevating our desires and our esteem above God's truth.

The next thing listed in II Timothy 3:2, immediately after lovers of self, is that people will be lovers of money. Jesus spoke in the gospels of this very thing. No one can serve two masters, for either he will hate the one and love the other or he will be devoted to the one and despise the other. You cannot serve God and money (Matthew 6:24). But those who desire to be rich fall into temptation, into a snare, into many senseless and harmful desires that plunge people into ruin and destruction. For the love of money is a root of all kinds of evils. It is through this craving that some have wandered away from the faith and pierced themselves with many pangs (I Timothy 6:9-10).

Is there corruption? Follow the money. It is at the heart of greedy, power-hungry individuals. I do not suggest that if you have money, you have given into evil. No! God apportions His resources as He sees fit. We all have different roles to play in God's kingdom;

therefore, some have more, some have less, and some have much less. The problems enter when we start to imagine ourselves the possessors of it rather than the stewards we actually are.

In some cases, the LORD may be asking you to sell all that you have and follow Him, but this will not be everyone's calling. We must refrain from measuring and comparing our lives against one another, for a man who measures himself by another has no understanding (II Corinthians 10:12). God has uniquely called us to specific walks of life and specific incomes, or lack thereof, to fulfill His purposes. We must learn contentment and seek the LORD's will over and above our own. But godliness with contentment is great gain, for we brought nothing into the world, and we cannot take anything out of the world, but if we have food and clothing, with these we will be content (I Timothy 6:6-8).

I am grateful to know the reality of utter dependence on God through the stripping of things and money. We are all completely dependent upon Him for everything, but with money, it is easy for me to become distracted by it. It is easy for me to act as if I am dependent upon it instead of on God. It is easy for me to fall prey to the illusion that I am somehow deserving of the credit and may do with it whatever I please. Beware lest you say in your heart, my power and the might of my hand have gotten me this wealth. You shall remember the LORD your God, for it is He who gives you the power to get wealth (Deuteronomy 8:17-18). Likewise, Hosea 2:5, 8 may strike a chord for some of you: For she said, I will go after my lovers who give me my bread and my water, my wool and my flax, my oil and my drink . . . And she did not know it was I (the LORD), who gave her the grain, the wine, and the oil and who lavished on her silver and gold which they used for [idol worship]. I know this certainly cut to my heart when I first read it.

God alone is our sufficiency. Nothing we steward comes from ourselves. Yet, the world and the ruler of this world would like you to believe otherwise. I see a terrible thing taking place in this land of independence and so-called self-sufficiency. I fell into this prideful trap of illusion myself. However, every good and perfect gift comes from above, coming down from the Father of lights (James 1:17). None of us can or should take any credit for anything. All we have comes from God – All. A person cannot receive even one thing unless it is given him from heaven (John 3:27). We are undeniably dependent upon Him for all of our needs. This really is a marvelous thing once we accept and submit to it.

I wonder how much different our lives would look if we began to make decisions based on the building of God's kingdom instead of the building of our bank accounts. The LORD provides for His people. He always has, and He always will. We are not to worry about what we will eat, drink, or wear and yet . . . we do. A motto I adopted early on in my journey is this: If I need it, He will provide it. If I don't have it, I don't need it.

We have seemingly lost sight of building God's kingdom in exchange for building our own kingdoms. How many of you are feeling anxious right now over the possible loss of what you consider to be comfortable? The idol of comfort sure has been a struggle in my own life. Why do we worry at all when the LORD has promised to fill our every need? Maybe we are putting our wants into the needs bucket, and we worry God may allow us to become uncomfortable. We worry that He may take from us the things in which we have come to find a false sense of security and happiness.

As we head deeper into a world being prepared to accept the one-world government and the mark of the beast, I implore you to lay down that idol called comfort at the feet of the Lord Jesus Christ and ask Him to give you trust and contentment. Remind yourself that no matter what He allows into your life or what he takes out of it, He will give you the strength and the grace necessary to walk through it. Remember, we serve a God who does the impossible. He rained bread from heaven, He used birds to deliver two meals a day, He fed thousands with one small lunch, and He multiplied the poor widow's flour and oil for two years past the point at which it was supposed to run out. He has got your back; of this you can be certain.

Another idol I wanted to touch base on is one I believe the least likely to be expected for most people. This is the way we seek to feed our prideful ego by way of religious activity and good works (aka ministry or outreach). Some people may be aware that they are serving with an impure motivation; others may be completely unaware. It takes the LORD's revelation to see ourselves more clearly. This is why we see David asking for this very revelation in Psalm 139. Search me, O God, and know my heart! Try me and know my thoughts! And see if there be any grievous (wicked, KJV) way in me and lead me in the way everlasting (the ancient way)!

Here is the truth. We are easily deceived, and the heart is deceitful above all things and desperately sick; who can understand it? (Jeremiah 17:9). Do not follow your heart as the world suggests. You will be led astray every time. Immerse yourself in God's Word and follow His truth. This idolatry is a little more abstract because from

the outside, serving the LORD looks much the same whether the mo-
tive is pure or self-seeking. Due to our desperately sick hearts, this
may not be easily discerned. We absolutely should devote time to
serving, and the LORD has already prepared works in which we will
walk, but we must ask God to search our hearts often, so that we do
not fall prey to this sneaky idolatry. Our pride is no joke, and it must
not be taken lightly.

We can idolize ministry and the way serving makes us feel about
ourselves. It is also possible to participate in ministry/outreach acting in our own strength. This will inevitably be a fruitless ministry
that will eventually lead to burnout and may even cause resentment
toward those whom you are supposed to be helping. We are, no
doubt, called to minister to others, but we should only be doing so
at the LORD's direction and in His strength. Only through abiding in
Him will we bear much fruit. We have heard it said, only that which
is done *for* Christ will last. The more accurate statement is this: Only
that which is done *through* Christ will last. Remember, there is a lot of
busyness that adds up to nothing.

In many cases, the focus has become ministry and outreach,
but this should never be the focus. Our churches ought not center
themselves around outreach ministries but around true discipleship
through the Word of God. People have needs, and we should live with
hands wide open, but this is not the foundation upon which to build
our churches. Additionally, what good is it to feed the belly if we are
not also nourishing the soul? What good is it if we are clothing the
body if we are not teaching them to be spiritually clothed? As the
body of Christ, we certainly do play a role as His hands and feet, and

we certainly should help those who are in need as we are able and as the LORD leads, but this should never be the foundation or purpose.

We can become fixated upon "doing for Jesus," "winning souls for Jesus," etc., but these are not the goals of the Christian. The goal is not to meet the needs of people but to be true to our relationship with the Lord Jesus Christ and to His will. Oswald Chambers says it this way: "The goal of the missionary is to do God's will, not to be useful or win the lost. A missionary is useful and does win the lost but that is not his goal. His goal is to do the will of His LORD" (*My Utmost for His Highest* by Oswald Chambers, edited by James Reimann, September 23 entry).

Be careful that you do not get distracted by your own usefulness for God. He does not need any one of us to achieve His purposes. We must not think more highly of ourselves than we ought (Romans 12:3). It is not about us. It is not about what we accomplish. It is not about our productivity. It is about Him. Our purpose is never to do "something that matters" for God. Our purpose is to be one with God through Christ, and He will do through us all that His heart intends. Moreover, it is not so much about what we are doing for Him as it is about what He is doing *in* us.

The next topic I would like to touch upon may be a sensitive subject for some, but I feel compelled to speak about cellphones; and I am going to share with you the personal conclusion I have drawn and my reasons for living without one (by the grace of God) for the past few years.

Initially, I ditched my phone because I was under such heavy surveillance I could not make it out safely if I held onto it. I could tell you of some experiences that would make you scratch your head.

However, I would come to know a much better reason to live without it. Shortly after we fled, I began to read the Bible, as you know. By the time I had finished reading it for the first time, I was positive the LORD did not want me to use a phone anymore, not because He could not keep me safe, but because it became obvious to me the idol it truly is.

You may want to debate with me at this point, saying technology is not evil; look at all the good the LORD has accomplished with it. I do not deny any of the good that has come from it, especially when it comes to Bible translation. Nevertheless, I would gently remind you that it has always been God's way to use what the enemy has meant for evil to accomplish His good purposes. This does not mean it is not detestable in His sight.

Please keep in mind, I am not sharing any of this with the idea that you ought to follow in my footsteps, doing what I have done, scattering them as unclean things, saying to them, be gone! (Isaiah 30:22, 2:20, and 31:6). That is exclusively between you and God. Therefore, my beloved, work out your own salvation with fear and trembling (Philippians 2:12). It is also obvious to me that, for some of you, it is necessary for the calling to which you have been called. Again, we are without understanding if we measure ourselves by one another. There is only one thing we ought to measure ourselves by, and this is the Word of God.

Shortly after we fled, I was skimming through a secular book about government. I do not remember the name of the book, but there was a short sentence that grabbed my attention. It said, the aim of technology was to put everything everyone ever said on a microdot and call it "god." Since the beginning of time, it has been the enemy's desire to be God, and he makes every effort to mimic Him in a twisted and perverted way. The enemy covets the attributes which belong to God alone, and he aspires to be omnipotent (all-powerful), omniscient (all-knowing), and omnipresent (all-present). It is not hard to see how the enemy uses technology to mimic these things. The scriptures are full of references to idols which cannot see, hear, or talk. I see this as the enemy's way of trying to do this very thing – Create an idol which can "see," "hear," "talk," and even "think" in a counterfeit way. We know the whole world lies in the power of the evil one, but have you ever considered why he is called the prince of the power of the air? I suggest that particular title has much to do with the transfer of information and data through the air.

Interestingly, Yuval Noah Harari recently made statements worth noting. Yuval Noah Harari is Chief Advisor to Klaus Schwab, Founder and Director of the World Economic Forum. On August 18, 2022, Harari declared, "We don't need some God in the clouds handing down tablets because we've created our own clouds and our own tablets." He also stated something which I have been saying for years, "If you have a problem in life, you don't ask God, you ask Google or Facebook." His direct quote is, "Data, and the ability to analyze data, is the new source of authority. If you have a problem in life, whether it is what to study, whom to marry or whom to vote for, you don't ask God above or your feelings inside, you ask Google or Facebook."

I see technology as a universal language that spans the whole earth. Do you recall the last time a universal language spanned the whole earth? That's right. It was the tower of Babel. Here is an interesting side note. My son pointed to a cell tower one day, and he said, "Eww, Mom, the tower of Babel!" Another day, he called it the tower of Babylon. Both are correct. That thought had never even crossed my mind, but he is right. In Genesis 11:6, the LORD said, "Behold, they are one people, and they have all one language, and this is only the beginning of what they will do. And nothing that they propose to do will now be impossible for them."

There are many ways in which technology has aided those who wish to mimic God. Whether they are manipulating food, water, weather, genes, our lives, our bodies, our minds, etc., it is all heading in one direction, the fulfillment of Revelation, and it is heading there fast. Again, Harari states something along these very lines. The interviewer asks, "You've predicted that humans could achieve a sort of divine state through biological manipulation or genetic engineering. How will that evolution happen?" Harari states, "This isn't a poetic metaphor or a vague metaphysical claim. It is a concrete prediction. Throughout history, humans have ascribed to gods specific abilities, such as to design and create living beings; to reshape their own bodies; to control the environment and the weather; to read minds and to communicate instantly across space; and to escape death and live indefinitely." One day, my daughter pointed to an Apple logo and said, "Eww, Mom, Adam and Eve." It is interesting that a symbol of forbidden knowledge was chosen, is it not? Technology is not neutral.

When I first realized God was asking me to step out into the unknown, in faith, and without a phone, I wondered how I would function. How would I get around without a GPS and bus schedules? God reminded me how He led the Israelites, and I had the distinct impression that He would lead me. He has faithfully done so. I thought, how will I get up in the morning without an alarm? The LORD impressed upon me that He would wake me up, and He does. I could tell you story after story of God's miraculous and faithful guidance and the huge blessing it has been. It has truly grown my faith, my love, and my trust in Him. Be assured, if the LORD does ask us to do something, He will give us the ability to carry out His plan for our lives in obedience to Him.

God did not flippantly choose the words which are written in His Word. The terminology is as intentional as He is. To me, it is impossible to ignore these terms when it comes to the subject of idols and idolatry (as I believe it relates to our use of phones today). These include, but are not limited to, the following:

- They bow down to the work of their hands and fingers – The typical posture for using a phone is bowed down.
- Gold plated metal images, overlaid with gold and silver – Ever notice the gold and silver inside of your phone?
- Images, metal images, carved images – He could have used many other words such as statue, figure, or sculpture, but He chose *images*.
- They lift it to their shoulders, they carry it, they set it in its place, it stands there – The first time I read this, my jaw dropped.
- Following their stubborn hearts and their own evil devices, the fruit of their devices . . .
- The images are false, worthless, a work of delusion – Social media anyone?
- But they continued to worship on the high places, the high places were not taken down. They sacrificed on tops of mountains and burned offerings on the hills – Over and over, the OT speaks of worship on the high places, which was an abomination detestable to the LORD. Ever notice where the cell towers are located? In high

places such as mountains, hills, tall towers, etc. The way that information is transferred, I cannot help but see this as worship on the high places.

- They stoop, they bow down together . . . they go into captivity – Do you live in captivity to your phone?
- Inquire of an idol – People inquire of their phone instead of God.
- The household gods utter nonsense – Google Home, Alexa, etc.

The scriptures from which these terms come are as follows:

- Their land is filled with idols. They bow down to the work of their hands, to what their own fingers have made (Isaiah 2:8).
- They are turned back and utterly put to shame who trust in carved idols, who say to the metal images, you are our gods (Isaiah 42:17).
- Their idols are on beasts and livestock. These things you carry are borne as burdens on weary beasts. They stoop. They bow down together. They cannot save the burden but themselves go into captivity (Isaiah 46:1-2).
- Then they fall down and worship. They lift it to their shoulders. They carry it. They set it in its place, and it stands there. It cannot move from its place. If one cries to it, it does not answer or save him from trouble (Isaiah 46:7).
- I spread out my hands all the day to a rebellious people who walk in a way that is not good, following their own devices, a people who provoke me to my face continually (Isaiah 65:2-3).
- Is the LORD not in Zion? Is her king not in her? Why have they provoked me to anger with their carved images and with their foreign idols? (Jeremiah 8:19).

- Every goldsmith is put to shame by his idols for his images are false and there is no breath in them. They are worthless, a work of delusion (Jeremiah 10:14-15, repeated 51:17-18).
- For it is a land of images and they are mad over their idols (Jeremiah 50:38).
- Therefore, the days are coming when I will punish the images of Babylon (Jeremiah 51:47).
- All worshipers of images are put to shame, who make their boast in worthless idols (Psalm 97:7).
- My people inquire of a piece of wood and their walking staff gives them oracles for a spirit of whoredom has led them astray, and they have left their God to play the whore. They sacrifice on the tops of mountains and burn offerings on the hills (Hosea 4:12-13).
- Repent and turn away from your idols and turn away your faces from all your abominations (Ezekiel 14:6).
- And I said to them, cast away the detestable things your eyes feast on, every one of you, and do not defile yourselves with the idols of Egypt (Ezekiel 20:7).
- I will destroy the idols and put an end to the images (Ezekiel 30:13).
- What profit is an idol? A metal image, a teacher of lies? For its maker trusts in his own creation when he makes speechless idols. Woe to him who says to a wooden thing, awake! And to a silent stone, arise! Can this teach? Behold, it is overlaid with gold and silver and there is no breath at all in it (Habakkuk 2:18-19).
- For the household gods utter nonsense (Zechariah 10:2).
- Behold, they are all a delusion. Their works are nothing. Their metal images are empty wind (Isaiah 41:29).

- They provoked Him to anger with their high places, they moved Him to jealousy with their idols (Psalm 78:58).

Our God says to us, more than once, you shall not worship me the way the surrounding nations worship; learn not the way of the nations, and yet . . .

Though it has been my calling to live without this device, I fully realize it may not be yours. In fact, as previously stated, you may have a calling on your life wherein it is necessary for the work He has called you to do.

Yet, for some of you, He may be speaking to your heart right now, asking you to refrain from or substantially cut back on the time you have devoted to the use of your phone. Listen to Him. I wonder how different our lives would look, and I wonder how much better our mental health crisis would be if people would put down the phone and pick up the Bible. I wonder what would happen if we bypassed the endless scrolling of images and replaced it with time spent in the presence of God.

How many of you are frantic if you do not have your phone near you, on you, in your hands? On the flipside, how many of you are desperate to have the Word of God near you, on you, in your hands? What if you could not leave the house without your Bible the same way you cannot leave the house without your phone? We have made a ton of sacrifices in the name of convenience and instant gratification, and we are reaping the "benefits" (disaster) of the unfaithfulness we have sown.

Another way we sacrifice to idols is by way of looking to things which promise immediate escape or relief from pain, heartache, boredom, and many other uncomfortable emotions. We have traded seeking the LORD's comfort and healing for indulgence in the passions of the flesh with things like alcohol, sex, food, drugs, entertainment, etc. We need to come to our senses, repent, and return to the LORD with our whole heart!

Another quite nefarious idolatry sweeping the nation is the idol of sensuality. There is a seducing spirit alive and extremely active in our present-day culture, and Christians are "giving heed to seducing spirits and teachings of demons." I did. I always wondered why the Bible talked of sensuality and sexual immorality as two different things. It seemed to me they were one and the same. I could not have been more wrong. Here is an example of where we see this. Now the works of the flesh are evident: sexual immorality, impurity, sensuality, idolatry, sorcery, enmity, strife, jealousy, fits of anger, rivalries, dissensions, divisions, envy, drunkenness, orgies, and things like these. I warn you, as I warned you before, that those who do such things will not inherit the kingdom of God (Galatians 5:19-21).

Sensuality is the pursuit of physical pleasure, and to be sensual refers to experience through the senses. This feel-good experience/sensuality is a big part of the music that entangled me. Additionally, there are many people who are speaking of their spiritual and supernatural experiences. We inherently know that there is more to life than this physical, natural world, so we are drawn to supernatural, spiritual things which we sense to be greater than ourselves. The enemy knows this. I am not saying we cannot have meaningful and even mind-blowing spiritual and supernatural experiences with God Almighty. Of course we can, and we do; I have. The question is, should we be talking about them?

I recently read part of a book called *How the Spirit Filled My Life* by Missionary Bertha Smith, and one line really grabbed my attention. She said, something to the effect of, be careful in speaking of your experiences. I thought that was odd because it was my understanding that we are supposed to tell others what God has done in our lives for His glory. As I was writing this book, I certainly kept out the moments that I was sure were meant for me and Him only, but I put in a couple of others that I thought would be okay to share. However, there is a counterfeit at work in the world of spirituality. There is a seducing spirit preying on the feel-good experience of the senses and our carnal desire for sensuality. They are calling this spirit the Holy Spirit, and people think it must be real because . . . it is. However, it is not the Holy Spirit at work as is claimed. It is something else entirely. It is counterfeit. It is dangerous. It is leading people astray.

In light of these recent revelations, I was compelled to edit and completely remove things from this book as I do not wish to mislead anyone. Tragically, it is possible to chase after the idol of sensuality through music, meditation, experience, and other means thinking you are connecting to God Almighty when really all you are doing is connecting to the underworld cloaked in so-called "light." Please be careful. If then the light in you is darkness, how great is the darkness! (Matthew 6:23b).

The enemy is a counterfeit, and if we would open our eyes (God, please open our eyes) to see how he is moving in all of these counterfeit ways, we may not be so apt to go along with all that we are told we *should* do. He will seek to deceive even the elect (true believers) and, sadly, he is already having much success.

We must humble ourselves and ask God to wipe our slate of so-called knowledge that is of the world. Let us leave that behind and seek the LORD with our whole heart in search of His pure truth and wisdom from above. The wisdom of this world is folly with God; let no one deceive himself. If anyone among you thinks he is wise in this age, let him become a fool that he may become wise (I Corinthians 3:18-19). I do not speak these words from a high and lofty place. Rather, I know how easily deceived I have been and can be, and to anyone who thinks he stands, take heed lest he fall (1 Corinthians 10:12). For many years, I lived as a believer deceived on many levels about who God is, about who I was, and about all that is going on in the world. Spoiler alert – Nothing is as it seems; nothing is as they tell you . . . nothing.

It is true I had God-given discernment at a young age, but as I continued in my disobedience and rebellion, my heart became hard and my mind became dull. They are darkened in their understanding, alienated from the life of God because of *the ignorance that is in them, due to their hardness of heart* (Ephesians 4:18, italics added). If this happens, we open wide the door for further and more consequential deceptions. When God reveals truth to us, we must respond in obedience to that truth, no matter how much it seems to cost us, no matter how deeply it humiliates our pride.

To this day, the LORD continues to reveal to me deception and hidden idolatries that must be eradicated in my life. When the LORD began to reveal the deception and lies to which I had fallen prey, I said in my alarm, all mankind are liars (Psalm 116:11). Praise be to the LORD, surrender and submission to Him and to His Word have brought, and are bringing, me into a deeper knowledge of the truth and a heavenly wisdom, resulting in closer fellowship with my Savior.

I mentioned previously that it is written there is another "Jesus" being proclaimed, and I never quite understood what Paul meant by "another Jesus." There are several ways this is happening. In one of these scenarios, there is some mythological history which sheds some light. It is written, take no part in the unfruitful works of darkness, but instead expose them (Ephesians 5:11).

Everything that God does, Satan imitates in a twisted and perverted way . . . everything. This includes the birth, death, and resurrection of Jesus Christ. This false christ is a false god, who has gone by many names throughout time, and of course the enemy is behind it all. The mythology behind this false god is complex, and quite frankly I do not want to go into all of it in much detail, but he is mentioned in the Bible as Tammuz. And he said to me, "Son of man, do you see what they are doing, the great abominations that the house of Israel are committing here, to drive me far from my sanctuary? But you will see still greater abominations" (Ezekiel 8:6). Then he brought me to the entrance of the north gate of the house of the LORD, and behold, there sat women weeping for Tammuz (Ezekiel 8:14).

There are slightly varying stories, but the undertone in all of them is the same. He is one part of an unholy trinity and a son who is a reincarnate of his father born to a supposed virgin. There are other twisted similarities such as the thought that he was a shepherd deity, who then became viewed as the power in the grain dying when the grain was milled. We know the Good Shepherd (Jesus Christ) stated, "Truly, truly, I say to you, unless a grain of wheat falls into the earth and dies, it remains alone; but if it dies, it bears much fruit" (John

12:24). This ancient Babylon mystery religion, this cult of Tammuz, bled into all cultures. The names changed, the face changed, but at its core it was always worship of Lucifer. This unholy trinity is seen in Egypt under the guise of Osiris, Isis, and Horus. We see it in worship of the sun, moon, and stars, and the list goes on and on. Underlying all of it is one false god – Lucifer. So why am I telling you all of this? Because we have all been led astray, and the Bible says, my people are destroyed for lack of knowledge (Hosea 4:6).

After my complete surrender, now three years ago, God immediately began pointing out and asking me to eliminate idolatry from my life. This took on many forms, as idolatry takes on many forms, but one of those things He asked me to cease was the celebration of Christmas. I had known for years that it is a holiday with deep pagan (Satanic) roots and traditions. The decorated trees, lights, wreaths, mistletoe, holly, eggnog, caroling, Santa and reindeer, fruitcakes, gifts under the tree, etc. originate entirely from pagan rituals and symbolism. This is not harmless; it is Satanic. However, I enjoyed it and justified my reasons for celebrating it, that is, until I became obedient to the LORD.

You may be thinking, hold on, wait a minute, we're celebrating the birth of Christ. Yes, that is what we have been led to believe. However, the birth of Christ did not take place in winter nor are we told in the Bible to celebrate His birth. The ugly truth is that December 25th is the recognized birthday of Tammuz, the false christ. In fact, we see this story replayed in Egyptology. It was believed that Horus, the son of Isis (the Egyptian name for the queen of heaven mentioned in the Bible) was born on December 25th, and thus his birthday was celebrated by pagans for centuries. This is the birthday of the false christ (the other "Jesus"), not the Christ Jesus that true Christians worship.

Christmas is not Christian. It is unequivocally pagan (Satanic). So why do so many Christians celebrate it? This deception dates back to around 336 A.D. during the reign of Constantine. His "conversion" and influence continues to profoundly affect our lives today. However, you cannot make something acceptable in the eyes of God simply by calling it Christian, and not everyone who calls themselves a Christian has been truly transformed by being born again. It is clear that, after his "conversion" he was still worshiping other deities. Throughout his life, he acknowledged Sol Invictus, the "unconquered sun" as a god.

Anytime there is sun imagery . . . think Lucifer, which means light bearer. Sun worship, goddess worship, and also mother/child worship is a prevalent theme throughout all pagan religions across time and, yes, this includes the Mary/Jesus worship of Catholicism. It all comes from the ancient system of Babylon, and it is Lucifer behind it all. [Goddess worship and mother/child worship are just additional facets of sun worship, which is Luciferian worship].

Constantine did declare that Christians could now worship freely, but he proceeded to erect pagan temples and statues in his new city, Constantinople. He declared the persecution of Christians cease, yes, but his personal devotions were offered to Mars and Apollo. Christianity did not infiltrate Rome . . . paganism infiltrated Christianity. He did not cease his pagan (Satanic) rituals. He simply called them Christian. It does not make it so. In fact, it makes all the sense in the world that Satan would choose to go about it in this way. For such men are false apostles, deceitful workmen, disguising themselves as apostles of Christ. And no wonder, for even Satan disguises himself as an angel of light (II Corinthians 11:13-14).

In the hours leading up to His sacrifice on the cross, Jesus Christ said, "Do this in remembrance of me," as He broke bread with His disciples. He did not ask us to remember His birthday; hence, we do not even know exactly when that took place, though we do know it was definitely not in the wintertime. We are not given this information because He never intended for us to memorialize Him as a helpless babe but, rather, as the conquering and risen Savior that He is.

This brings me into my next uncomfortable topic . . . Easter. I found out about the heresy of Easter years ago back in the early 2000s, and at the prompting of the Holy Spirit, I stopped doing all the pagan things I grew up with like painting eggs, egg hunts, bunnies, and the like, but I could not convince my own mom about the heresy of these holidays. She would say, "Well, I am doing it for Jesus, and God knows my heart," but we cannot slap the name Christian on something and call it acceptable worship of God Almighty.

Easter, in fact, was originally (and still is) the celebration of Ishtar, Assyrian and Babylonian goddess of fertility and sex; hence, fertility and sex symbols like the egg and the bunny are used. The ancient Sumerian legend surrounding this celebration is actually a blasphemous resurrection story of its own. In short, Tammuz, married to Ishtar, dies. Ishtar follows him to the underworld griefstricken. There she is judged, killed, and hung on display. The earth loses its fertility, crops cease, and animals stop reproducing. Ishtar goes missing for three days when her assistant seeks help from other gods. One of them goes to the underworld and gives Tammuz and

Ishtar the power to return to the earth as the light of the sun for six months.

I do not mean to convey that these myths and legends actually took place. They are, however, the stories concocted by the enemy, and they are the back stories for the pagan rituals, customs, and idolatry practiced. At the very heart of it all is only one thing – Worship of Lucifer, the false christ.

I realize the King James Version uses the word Easter in Acts 12:4. And when he had apprehended him, he put him in prison, and delivered him to four quaternions of soldiers to keep him; intending after Easter to bring him forth to the people. Though I have my own theory on why this is the case, I will not speculate to you in writing. Nevertheless, it is important to note that in the original Greek the word is *pascha*. This word should be translated Passover.

When a cross is put on the forehead in celebration of Ash Wednesday, that is a T or a Tau for Tammuz. The weeping for Tammuz, which God castigates as abomination in Ezekiel, corresponds with the forty days of Lent practiced today. As the legend goes, in short, Tammuz's mother (a Babylonian "goddess" referred to as the queen of heaven in the Bible) called for forty days of fasting and weeping for her son. And behold, there sat women weeping for Tammuz (Ezekiel 8:14b). Lent is not a Biblical practice, but it does line up with the Muslim's observance of Ramadan. Biblically speaking, we are to remember Christ's death, burial, and resurrection at the time of Passover and the Feast of Unleavened Bread. Remembering the Lord's sacrifice, Biblically, is a feast . . . not a fast.

This mixing of ancient Babylonian paganism and Christianity is detestable in the eyes of God. The argument that we can, in fact, adopt these evil practices and turn them into acceptable worship by "Christianizing" them is false. God specifically speaks out against this: Take care that you be not ensnared to follow them, after they have been destroyed before you, and *that you do not inquire about their gods, saying, 'How did these nations serve their gods?—that I also may do the same.' You shall not worship the* LORD *your God in that way, for every abominable thing that the* LORD *hates they have done for their gods*, for they even burn their sons and their daughters in the fire to their gods (Deuteronomy 12:30-31, italics added).

All of God's children across every denomination have been guilty of idolatry and practicing paganism – All of us. It is time to wake up! We are in desperate need of a reformation, and we will not see true, undefiled revival until reformation takes place in the hearts of individuals. If my people who are called by my name humble themselves and pray and seek my face and turn from their wicked ways, then I will hear from heaven and will forgive their sin and heal their land (II Chronicles 7:14).

We need to realize that we have been deceived into mimicking the ways of the heathen nations, and God is not at all pleased. Christmas, Easter, and the false Sabbath (which was originally proclaimed as a day of sun worship – Hence, the name Sun-day) are just a few of the many hundreds of ways we have been duped into following man's commands, doctrine, and opinion while completely straying from the Word of God. We have become corrupt. God Almighty is calling His remnant out of this false and worldly system we now call Christianity. Modern Christianity is not Biblical Christianity, and we need to immerse ourselves in the scriptures and adhere solely to God's Word once again. God tells us in His Word many times that we are not permitted to worship Him in the way the pagan peoples worship their gods (see Deuteronomy 12:4 and others).

We are right and in line with God's Word to celebrate His death and resurrection but not by mimicking the way of the godless nations. Just as we can do the right thing for the wrong reason, we can do the right thing the wrong way. God actually put it in my heart to celebrate Passover with my children the past few years. We do not honor Passover according to Jewish custom and tradition, but we have celebrated it in the way in which God has led according to His Word, and it has been a real blessing, indeed. If you have never studied the seven feasts of God, I would encourage you to do so. Jesus Christ died on Passover and was raised on the Feast of Firstfruits. The Holy Spirit was given on the Feast of Weeks (Pentecost), and He will fulfill the last three feasts once He returns. That was just a little side note, but these celebrations are completely relevant to us today as Christians.

This information is not meant to attack any person as an individual; it is an attack on idolatry, which is a grievous sin and a grave unfaithfulness. We have all been lulled into accepting idolatry as a normal part of our lives. However, just as in the days of Josiah, we need to rediscover the Word of God and begin to tear down these idols one by one as they are revealed to us. I pray that this information sparks a desire to seek the wisdom that comes from God with all your heart, mind, soul, and strength. Call to me and I will answer you and will tell you great and hidden things that you have not known (Jeremiah 33:3).

You may recall a scripture that comes from Romans 14:5-6a: One person esteems one day as better than another, while another esteems all days alike. Each one should be fully convinced in his own mind. The one who observes the day, observes it in honor of the LORD. I had to wrestle through this verse with the LORD. I am confident today that the context of this scripture refers to those who celebrate the feasts of the LORD or other Jewish observances, not pagan feasts. Christians in Paul's day were not celebrating pagan holidays such as Christmas and Easter (this began in the fourth century). However, there were some who celebrated Jewish feasts and observances and some who did not.

If we use this scripture in Romans 14 to justify celebrating something as occultic as Christmas (I did), we are being led astray by a verse out of context. God never condones pagan-like worship nor idolatry – Never. In fact, He brings His judgment on His people because of it. You may be thinking, but there is therefore now no condemnation for those who are in Christ Jesus. Yes, true. However, judgment begins at the household of God (I Peter 4:17), and it happens here on earth. If the righteous is repaid on earth, how much more the wicked and the sinner (Proverbs 11:31). God is not mocked. We reap what we sow. If you have not felt the hand of God and His judgment befall you here on earth, it is not too late. Repent now and turn from your wicked ways. The LORD relents over disaster, and He desires to extend His mercy to us, but if we continue in our rebellion and refuse to repent, it is only a matter of time. For we know Him who said, "Vengeance is mine; I will repay." And again, "The LORD will judge *His* people." It is a fearful thing to fall into the hands of the living God (Hebrews 10:30-31).

To be clear, God's judgment of His people differs from the judgment that will befall those who reject Christ. God's judgment on *His* children is synonymous with His discipline. He disciplines those He loves, and it is always for our good and His glory. But if we judged (or discerned) ourselves truly, we would not be judged. But when we are judged by the LORD, we are disciplined so that we may not be condemned along with the world (I Corinthians 11:31-32).

Please do not think for a second that this is my way of pointing an angry finger at anyone. Of course I am in no position to even think about doing so. I have been called, however, to expose the unfruitful works of darkness and to point out some of the deceptions to which we have all fallen prey. God's name is greatly profaned when we call ungodly things godly, and we need to get back to the authority of God's Word and let go of the worldly influence. I say what I say not to convince you, not to change you, and not to condemn you. I say what I say to shine a light in the darkness. Whether these words of revelation are a catalyst for change or whether they are ignored is between you and God. My only purpose is to be obedient to what God has called me to do – To proclaim on the housetops what I have heard whispered (Matthew 10:27). I have not shared anything with you that I myself have not had to wrestle through in my own life and through the scriptures.

I know that none of this is easy to hear, and I know the struggle to break free from familiarity and tradition. Still, we have got to realize that, no matter how sincere we may be, God is not honored through our adulterous pagan practices, not even a little.

Be careful in believing that it is the motivation of your spirit which matters. Be careful in believing that God is pleased with pagan ritualism done in His name. Be careful in believing that He will accept your worship so long as you mean well. None of this is biblical.

To the contrary, our "worship" can be an abomination detestable in His sight if we are worshiping in opposition to His Word.

After the golden calf was fashioned at the foot of Mount Sinai, Aaron made a proclamation and said, "Tomorrow shall be a feast to the LORD" (Exodus 32:5). Of course, this was not pleasing to God, and we know thousands of them died in a plague. We are not so different from the Israelites. We have many "sacred cows" that we incorporate into our "worship" of the LORD. Christmas and Easter are the tip of the iceberg. The result is not God's glory and pleasure. The result is God's anger and judgment. Additionally, Nadab and Abihu offered unauthorized fire (unauthorized worship) and were struck dead (Leviticus 10:1-3), and Saul was stripped of his kingdom (I Samuel 13:8-14 and I Samuel 15:21-24) for refusing to stay within the confines of the commandments of God when it comes to worship.

They chose to worship God on their terms as opposed to worshiping God on His terms, and they incurred God's judgment because of it. It does not matter how sincere we may be or how pure we believe our motives to be if our "worship" is in direct contradiction with the Word of God. Let it not be said of us that we have a fine way of rejecting the commandments of God to keep the traditions of men in order to establish our tradition! (see Mark 7:7-9). It is a Pharisee (hypocrite) who practices strict adherence to tradition at the cost of obedience to God's Word.

Something I have heard often is this: Well, God knows my heart. Yes, God does know your heart, but do you know your heart? Do any of us really know our hearts? The heart is deceitful above all things, and desperately wicked: who can know it? (Jeremiah 17:9, KJV). Take care lest your heart be deceived, and you turn aside and serve other gods and worship them (Deuteronomy 11:16).

We look for and find ways to justify ourselves apart from scripture while ignoring the black and white instructions of His Word. This should not be the case. We need to cease following the ways of man and get back to living by *scripture alone*. A true fear of the LORD is sorely lacking in these last days, and we need to repent and return to Him. If we are confronted with the black and white truth of God's Word, through which the Holy Spirit convicts us, and we justify our actions based on our feelings, we have entered extremely dangerous territory behind enemy lines. The problem is that we do not want discipleship to cost us anything. We do not want to surrender our will to His. We do not want to conform to God's Word. We want God to conform to us.

It is true that our land is thoroughly saturated with idolatry to the point that we cannot be completely free of it. That does not mean we ought not be striving to rid our personal lives of it as the LORD leads us to do so. The past few years, I have found myself in a perpetual state of purging the things of this world and the idols from my heart. It is a process that is ever ongoing, as it should be. *It is not my focus, and it should not be yours.* Our gaze should be firmly fixed upon Christ alone. Nevertheless, He will definitely reveal in our hearts and minds when something has got to go.

We must stay sensitive to the voice of God by being obedient to His voice because how small a whisper do we hear of Him. Unfortunately, it is sometimes easy for us to ignore His faint whisper. This is detrimental to our spiritual health and our intimacy with Him. I cannot think of a time when it has been super easy to obey, but it is worth it. We may not be able to do something about everything, but we can do something about the next thing God reveals. He does not reveal everything to us all at once; we could not handle it. However, when He does see fit to reveal, there is only one sensible response . . . obedience. Striving to rid our lives of idolatry is not legalism; *it is loyalty.*

When it comes to the things of this world, my children and I live by this scriptural motto: If it causes you to sin, cut it off (or if you have become attached to it, cut it off). In obedience to the promptings of God, we have had to dispose of many things we have been given, either because it displayed idolatry in some way or because it had caused sin in our hearts. It used to greatly disturb my sensibilities to throw away new or perfectly good items, which I did not feel comfortable giving away. Then, one day I realized as I read God's Word that this was actually very common, and it was known as "devoting to destruction." Knowing and understanding this makes it much easier to do God's will as we must often devote to destruction the things of this world in order to honor God in faithfulness through obedience.

You may be thinking to yourself, is all of this purging necessary? I mean aren't we saved by God's grace through faith, which is not a result of works? Yes, that is absolutely true. Our works have nothing to do with our salvation or our standing before a righteous God, nothing, and *it is crucial that we fully grasp this truth*. However, our works have everything to do with the ability to grow and mature into intimate relationship with Him. What then? Are we to sin because we are not under law but under grace? By no means! (Romans 6:15).

We can "know" a lot about God without knowing Him at all. It is my prayer that everyone who reads this book may be given the Spirit of wisdom and of revelation in the knowledge of Him, having the eyes of your hearts enlightened (Ephesians 1:17-18a) because to know God intimately is a game changer. And by this we know that we have come to know him, if we keep his commandments. Whoever says "I know him" but does not keep his commandments is a liar, and the truth is not in him (I John 2:3-4).

We can get stuck in the place of infancy when it comes to our walk with God. I know it all too well as I lived in this place for more than thirty years. Sure, I had a victory here and there, and there was even some Bible study, prayer, and church, but something huge was missing – Complete surrender and unadulterated obedience. Without these, maturing into an intimate relationship with Christ will not take place. I did not completely surrender every aspect of my life into the hands of God. In the place of surrender sat pride, rebellion, and idolatry. I refused to heed the voice of God and the many warnings He gave. He is longsuffering, and He is patient, but there will come a point when He will put His foot down, so to speak. It is for His glory and for our good, but it is painful and it is devastating.

A refusal to voluntarily lay down our idols will result in a forceful and painful stripping of them. That could be a parent, spouse, or children; that could be a home or job; that could be possessions of all sorts or money; it could be anything. For me, it was all of the above, and He dealt a swift blow to remove it all, more than once, until I finally got a clue in my thick skull that life is not about the people and things of this world . . . It is about Him. It is all about Him, and it should be.

For anyone who does not know the intense hatred God has for idolatry in the lives of His children, please read your Bible! The way we whore after all these other "gods" is detestable in His sight. He has been patient, but we are at a huge crossroads. Will we continue to follow the course of this world or will we wake up to the deception and begin to break away from it? As obedient children, do not be conformed to the passions of your former ignorance, but as He who called you is holy, you also be holy in all your conduct, since it is written, "You shall be holy, for I am holy." . . . Knowing that you were ransomed from the futile ways inherited from your forefathers (I Peter 1:14-16, 18a).

Be doers of the Word and not hearers only, deceiving yourselves (James 1:22). James tells us that faith without works is dead. I used to think of works in terms only of social outreach type stuff as it speaks of helping a brother or sister poorly clothed and lacking in food, but he goes on to say, but someone will say, "You have faith and I have works." Show me your faith apart from your works, and I will show you my faith by my works. You believe that God is one; you do well. Even the demons believe – and shudder! Do you want to be shown, you foolish person, that faith apart from works is useless? Was not Abraham our father justified by works when he offered up his son Isaac on the altar? You see that faith was active along with his works, and faith was completed by his works (James 2:18-22). In speaking of the works of Abraham, he is speaking of obedience. Therefore, faith without obedience is dead/useless.

Obedience matters to God. It matters that we do as He tells us to do, whether that plays out in terms of giving to the needy, laying down an idol, or some other form of sacrifice. The times of ignorance God overlooked, but now He commands all people everywhere to repent (Acts 17:30). That they should repent and turn to God, performing deeds in keeping with their repentance (Acts 26:20b). Therefore let us leave the elementary doctrine of Christ and go on to *maturity*, not laying again a foundation of repentance from dead works and of faith toward God (Hebrews 6:1, italics added).

If you love me, you will keep my commandments (John 14:15). Little children, let us not love in word or talk but in deed and truth (I John 3:18). If I say to my husband, "I love you," and then commit adultery with another man, do I really love my husband? If I say to God, "I love you," and then commit spiritual adultery via idolatry, do I really love God? We are the beloved betrothed bride of Christ. We have got to take our separation from these wicked, adulterous practices more seriously. We have got to take God's Word and His warnings more seriously as well.

I implore you, dearly beloved child of God, do not conform to this world and do not love the world or the things of the world. Keep yourselves from idols! Pray this scripture, LORD, turn my eyes from looking at worthless things and give me life in your ways (Psalm 119:37).

When we gaze upon evil in acceptance and adoration, we turn our backs toward God. They have turned to me their back and not their face. And though I have taught them persistently, they have not listened to receive instruction. They set up their abominations in the house that is called by my name, to defile it (Jeremiah 32:33-34).

To turn *away* from evil. This is true understanding.

- If anyone loves the world, the love of the Father is not in them for all that is in the world – the desires of the flesh and the desires of the eyes and pride of life (pride in possessions) – is not from the Father but is from the world (I John 2:15-16).

- Then those of you who escape will remember me among the nations where they are carried captive, how I have been broken over their whoring heart that has departed from me and over their eyes that go whoring after their idols, and they will be loathsome in their own sight for the evils that they have committed, for all their abominations, and they shall know that I am the LORD (Ezekiel 6:9-10).
- And if it is evil in your eyes to serve the LORD, choose this day whom you will serve, whether the gods your fathers served in the region beyond the River, or the gods of the Amorites in whose land you dwell. But as for me and my house, we will serve the LORD (Joshua 24:15).
- So whoever knows the right thing to do and fails to do it, for him it is sin (James 4:17).
- Take care then how you hear. For to the one who has, more will be given, and from the one who has not, even what he thinks he has will be taken away (Luke 7:18).
- When God saw what they did, how they turned from their evil way, God relented of the disaster that he had said he would do to them, and he did not do it (Jonah 3:10).
- Abstain from all appearance of evil (I Thessalonians 5:22, KJV).
- Therefore, beloved, flee idolatry! (I Corinthians 10:14).

CHAPTER SEVEN

Now Go – The End of All Things is at Hand!

Blow a trumpet in Zion! Sound an alarm on my holy
mountain! Let all the inhabitants of the land tremble
for the day of the LORD is coming; it is near, a day of
darkness and gloom, a day of clouds and thick darkness
. . . Yet, even now, declares the LORD, return to me with
all your heart, with fasting, with weeping, and with
mourning, and rend your hearts and not your garments.
Return to the LORD your GOD for He is gracious and
merciful, slow to anger and abounding in steadfast love,
and He relents over disaster.

Joel 2:1-2, 12, 13

THERE ARE SOME OF you reading this book who already enjoy a close and intimate relationship with the LORD. The things I have been discovering over the past few years, He has been teaching you as well. There is an awakening going on in these last days. Praise the LORD! However, there may be some of you who are stuck where I was up until recently – Always learning, yet never able to arrive at a knowledge of the truth. Maybe you have been poorly shepherded and poorly discipled, if at all. Maybe you are, as I was, stubborn and unwilling to give up your illusion of control. Maybe it is a combination of things. Still, others may be wandering in a much more subtle way. You are honoring Him with your lips, but your heart is far from Him. Maybe you are so busy doing things *for* Him that you have neglected to make time to be *with* Him. Make no mistake, if you are a born-again believer in Christ Jesus, He is with you always, but are you with Him? Do you make time for your relationship with Him or is He often neglected and even at times ignored?

Some of you may be currently under conviction by the Spirit of God to surrender your life to Jesus Christ and follow Him. You have never made this commitment, but you would like to do so. There is no special formula. There are no certain words you must say. It is simply this – Believe in your heart that Jesus Christ died and rose again for you, taking the penalty of your sin upon Himself (the wages of our sin is death). Pour out your heart to God from a sincere heart of humility, confessing your sins to Him through whatever words He gives you to speak. Once this reconciliation takes place, you will be sealed by His Holy Spirit. Then *turn from your sin and your wicked ways* and seek the LORD with all your heart. It is only by the precious blood of Jesus Christ that we may be reconciled to God. There is no other way. Jesus Christ is The Way, The Truth, and The Life. No one comes to the Father except through Him (see John 14:6).

What a beautiful and wonderful gift. We are not only forgiven; we are invited into intimate relationship with our God. In His mercy, He does not give us what we deserve – Death and eternal separation from Him. By His grace, He gives us what we do not deserve

– Intimate relationship with Him, the greatest treasure of all. There is none like Him!

So, seek the LORD while He may be found. Call upon Him while He is near. Let the wicked forsake his way and the unrighteous man his thoughts. Let him return to the LORD that He may have compassion on him and to our God, for He will abundantly pardon! For my thoughts are not your thoughts neither are your ways my ways, declares the LORD. For as the heavens are higher than the earth, so are my ways higher than your ways and my thoughts than your thoughts (Isaiah 55:6-9).

To those who need to commit to the LORD for the first time, repent. To those who need to renew their covenant with the LORD because your apostasy has estranged you from the relationship, repent. To those who are walking closely with the LORD, pray and teach others to repent and disciple them to walk with the LORD in maturity.

I cannot say it enough. Time is running out, and we have been entrusted with the ministry of reconciliation. All this is from God, who through Christ reconciled us to Himself and gave us the ministry of reconciliation. That is, God was in Christ reconciling the world to Himself, not counting their trespasses against them and entrusting to us the message of reconciliation (II Corinthians 5:18-19). Are we fulfilling this calling as we ought?

God desires all people to be saved and to come to a knowledge of the truth (see I Timothy 2:4). Have we become so distracted that we have lost sight of what is truly important to our Savior? Have we become so self-absorbed that we barely care what will become of the lost? I think the answer is, yes. We lack a great deal of compassion, and I am the first one to admit it. Forgive us, LORD, and open our eyes to see what you see. For it is time for judgment to begin at the household of God, and if it begins with us, what will be the outcome for those who do not obey the gospel of God? If the righteous is scarcely saved, what will become of the ungodly and the sinner? (I Peter 4:17-18). I will tell you what will become of them. They will be thrown into the outer darkness where there is weeping and gnashing of teeth, and anyone's name not found written in the Lamb's Book of Life will be thrown into the Lake of Fire (Matthew 8:12 and Revelation 20:15). Yet, compassion seems oftentimes lacking, and so I pray, LORD, increase my compassion. Make me more like you.

If you think we have been living in dark times, it is about to get much darker. I wonder how many of us are truly ready for this. How many of us are desperately clinging to our relationship with God and to His Word? This is the only way to prepare our hearts and minds for what is coming. Watch and pray that you may not enter into temptation (Matthew 26:41a). Fortunately, light shines most brilliantly in the darkest of times, so in this we can rejoice, but it will not be without suffering and persecution. You will be hated by all for my sake, says Jesus Christ. You will have tribulation (Mark 13:13 and John 16:33).

I spent the majority of my life believing what I had heard so many preachers, books, and movies teach. I believed that Christians living on the earth will be plucked up out of the earth to go be with Jesus before it gets too treacherous. As I came to know the Word for myself, I realized I could not find any scripture which supports this idea. To the contrary, I read many scriptures contradicting it. It shocked me. Maybe it is shocking you right now. Maybe you would like to blow me off at this point. Please, hear me out. God has told us all things beforehand that we might not be caught off guard, but rather be fully prepared.

We know that Jesus Christ will return for a second time. We know that He will descend from Heaven with a cry of command with the voice of an archangel and with the sound of the trumpet of God, and the dead in Christ will rise first. Then we who are alive, who are left, will be caught up together with them in the clouds to meet the LORD in the air, and so we will always be with the LORD (I Thessalonians 4:16-17). At that time, yes, Christians will be plucked up, both dead and alive, but there is no biblical evidence to support that this will take place before we go through extensive suffering.

Though I do not believe we will be here when the bowls of wrath are poured out, I do not agree with the train of thought that the seven seals, seven trumpets, and seven bowls of wrath mentioned in the book of Revelation are all one and the same. My interpretation varies slightly. While it seems the trumpets and the bowls may possibly coincide, it seems to me that scripture clearly states that the seventh seal opens up the first trumpet. When the Lamb opened the seventh seal, there was silence in heaven for about half an hour. Then I saw the seven angels who stand before God, and seven trumpets were given to them (Revelation 8:1-2). Hence, we will go through significant chaos and persecution prior to being caught up in the air (see the seven seals in Revelation 6).

The first seal reveals the antichrist. I am not sure this will be widely discerned, but he will be revealed, nonetheless. In the second seal, people are permitted to slay one another. In the third seal, severe famine will ravage the world. In the fourth seal, one-quarter of the world's population will be killed by famine, pestilence, and sword. That is somewhere around two billion people. The fifth seal reveals the souls of those who had been slain for the Word of God, which I will further explore along with the sixth seal below. The LORD does not come back a second and a third time. He comes back for a second time only, so let us take a look now at some of the other scriptures surrounding this event.

Let no one deceive you in any way, for that day will not come unless the rebellion comes first and the man of lawlessness is revealed, the son of destruction, who opposes and exalts himself against every so-called god or object of worship, so that he takes his seat in the temple of God, proclaiming himself to be God . . . The Lord Jesus will kill him with the breath of His mouth and bring him to nothing by the appearance of His coming (II Thessalonians 2:3-4, 8). When this scripture mentions *that day* it is speaking of the return of the Lord Jesus Christ. When it mentions the *man of lawlessness*, we know this is the antichrist. We see quite clearly from this scripture alone that Christ does not return until after the rebellion and the reign of the antichrist. We see the same in Daniel. As I looked, this horn made war with the saints and prevailed over them *until* the Ancient of Days came! (Daniel 7:21).

In the fifth seal, we see the souls of those who had been slain for the Word of God and for the witness they had borne. They are crying out with a loud voice, "How long until you avenge our blood?" They were given a white robe and told to rest a little longer until the number of their fellow servants and brothers and sisters should be complete and were killed as they had been. At the sixth seal, there is a great earthquake and the sun becomes black, the moon becomes like blood, the stars fall to the earth, and the sky vanishes, rolling up like a scroll.

Mark 13:24-27 says, but in those days, *after* that tribulation, the sun will be darkened and the moon will not give its light and the stars will be falling from heaven, and the powers in the heavens will be shaken, and *then* they will see the Son of Man coming in the clouds with great power and glory. And *then* He will send out the angels and gather His elect from the four winds, from the ends of the earth, to the ends of heaven. So the LORD comes back after the sixth seal. By this time, we know that at least two billion people have died from famine, pestilence, and sword, and according to the fifth seal, many of us (Christians) have been persecuted and killed, and still more will be killed.

If we look into Revelation 13, we see the beast rising out of the sea with ten horns and seven heads. We see this in Daniel as well, and it is my interpretation that this will be the upcoming global government. According to verses 5-7, this beast will be allowed to exercise authority for forty-two months and allowed to *make war on the saints and to conquer them* (italics added).

According to Revelation 13:11-18, the second beast (which I interpret as the antichrist) exercises the authority of the first beast (which I interpret as the global government) and makes the earth and its inhabitants worship the first beast. This second beast deceives those who dwell on earth, telling them to make an image for the first beast and to cause those who will not worship the image of the beast to be slain and also causes everyone to be marked on the right hand or forehead so that no one can buy or sell unless he has the mark, which is what we call the mark of the beast. All these things take place prior to the return of Christ. Remember, the Lord Jesus will kill him (antichrist) with the breath of His mouth and bring him to nothing *by the appearance of His coming* (italics added).

By evidence of the scriptures, we will face famines, pestilence, and sword, and the first and the second beast will seek to destroy and will conquer us (Christians). We will be hated by all and killed for the witness we are for Christ and God's Word.

Are we ready for this? While I write this book from the U.S., I realize in many other parts of the world, my brothers and sisters are heavily persecuted and killed already for their faith in God. LORD, be near to them. But to those of us who have been without this level of persecution, either here or in other more tolerant parts of the world, are we ready for this? How do we get ready for this? We get ready by seeking depth in our relationship with God and by anchoring ourselves in the truth of God's Word. It is the only way. The enemy will seek to deceive even the elect. We must stay grounded in God's truth and in His love. So let us cling to the LORD and store His Word deep in our hearts before we no longer have easy access to it.

I am afraid there are far too many who remain unprepared even though the LORD God does nothing without revealing His secret to His servants, the prophets (Amos 3:7). It does not help that many are teaching that we will be zapped out of here before it gets too hard as they look to the Day of the LORD as something only glorious. Amos 5:18, 20 says, woe to you who desire the Day of the LORD! Why would you have the Day of the LORD? It is darkness and not light. It is gloom with no brightness in it. In Revelation 1:7, it says, behold, He is coming with the clouds and every eye will see Him, even those who pierced Him, and all tribes of the earth will wail (mourn) on account of Him. Why the wailing and the mourning? Because He is bringing His recompense (His vengeance) with Him. The return of the LORD is not a day of light but of gloom and darkness, and woe to him who desires this day.

It is not hard to see just how many pieces of this once puzzling puzzle are falling into place and are doing so quite rapidly. While it all remained quite far off and futuristic in times past, it is a lot more easily seen today how this may all go down in the not too distant future. Agenda 2030 seeks to have us operating under a one-world government by the year 2030, and the mark of the beast is well on its way as the technology is already being implemented in some countries, so . . . time is running out, and we are heading into some extremely dark and tumultuous times.

Get close to Christ Jesus and stay close. Be courageous and be willing to be different. I have faced plenty of ridicule over the past few years for refusing government handouts, but this does not hold a candle to the choice that the masses will be facing soon when it comes to acceptance or refusal of government handouts. We must dare to be different, especially in the face of ridicule, opposition, desperation, and persecution.

Since all these things are thus to be dissolved, what sort of people ought you to be in lives of holiness and godliness, waiting for and hastening the coming of the Day of God, because of which the heavens will be set on fire and dissolved and the heavenly bodies will melt as they burn! But according to His promise, we are waiting for new heavens and a new earth in which righteousness dwells. Therefore, beloved, since you are waiting for these, be diligent to be found by Him without spot or blemish and be at peace and count the patience of our LORD as salvation . . . Take care that you are not carried away with the error of lawless people and lose your own stability but grow in the grace and knowledge of our Lord and Savior, Jesus Christ. To Him be the glory both now and to the day of eternity. Amen (II Peter 3:11-18).

What comes to mind when you hear the phrase *the error of lawless people*? Who do you think of when you envision lawlessness? Perhaps thieves and murderers and the like? I would like to put forth another thought as we look at the error of lawless people. The antichrist himself is named the man of lawlessness, and we know that the deception of the antichrist will be cloaked in what appears to be good. He will be given power to perform many signs and wonders, and he will usher in a deceptive appearance of peace. Though he will be extremely violent toward real Christians, could it be possible that he may even claim to be a Christian himself? It would not surprise me. This deception has been around for thousands of years, and it is certainly prevalent in today's world. There are many wolves out there calling themselves Christians, who are, in fact, children of lawlessness (children of Satan).

I wrote briefly about another "Jesus" being preached. This is happening in several different ways, and if you do not intimately know God and His Word, deception is imminent and well under way. It is impossible to spot these deceptions without God's Spirit and discernment working in you because it is so cloaked in Christian language and "good" works. Jesus is painted in a positive light and scripture is quoted, and that is how the enemy gets us. He uses mostly truth with enough of a twist of perversion that we are completely thrown off track, if not utterly destroyed.

The allure is most commonly not the dark and sadistic type, though it is for some; for most, the allure is a masquerade of light. Evil does not always appear evil. Make no mistake, Jesus said, "Whoever is not with me is against me, and whoever does not gather with me scatters" (Luke 11:23 and Matthew 12:30). There are only two choices for "religion" in this world. You are either for God Almighty of the Bible (Father, Son, and Holy Spirit) or you are for Lucifer, the devil. While the enemy may have many different forms of religion that he is operating under, the truth is there are only two.

The enemy is the master counterfeiter, and deception is running rampant. We need to be alert and on guard in these last days. We need to cling to the LORD and to His Word. In Matthew 13:24-30, Jesus tells a parable of the weeds sown among the wheat by the enemy. In the KJV, the word "weeds" is translated "tares." The thing about a tare is that it looks just like wheat as it grows along with it. You can only spot the counterfeit upon close examination and inspection of its fruit (the grain). The enemy counterfeits all that is good and all that is godly. And no wonder, for even Satan disguises himself as an angel of light (II Corinthians 11:14). Be. On. Guard.

The true gospel is the preaching of grace through faith in the blood of Jesus Christ and forgiveness of sins through repentance. Repentance includes turning from our sin and our wicked ways. Instead, we are seeing a massive uptick in the preaching of grace and acceptance of our sin. Afterward Jesus found him in the temple and said to him, "See, you are well! Sin no more, that nothing worse may happen to you" (John 5:14). This false teaching that God's grace is a stamp of approval for the sin from which we do not want to turn away is from the father of lies.

Additionally, in an attempt to make Christianity "more palatable" to the lost, the church has for centuries allowed pagan traditions and worldly thoughts, ideas, and music to creep in. We are reaping what has been sown . . . corruption. To quote Charles Spurgeon, "I believe that one reason why the church of God at this present time has so little influence over the world is because the world has so much influence over the church." Of this I am certain; it is despicable in the eyes of God. He has all the power to draw people to Himself and to His church, but He requires us to be a people set apart, not a people of conformity. Training us to renounce ungodliness and worldly passions, and to live self-controlled, upright, and godly lives in the present age (Titus 2:12). As I stated in the previous chapter, we are in dire need of a reformation. Then I heard another voice from heaven saying, "Come out of her, my people, lest you take part in her sins, lest you share in her plagues" (Revelation 18:4).

In many cases, the church has been putting doctrine aside for the sake of "unity." The problem with putting doctrine aside for the sake of "unity" is that when you put doctrine aside, you put the Word of God aside. If you put the Word of God aside, you have certainly achieved unity, but it is not of God, and it is not Christian whether you call it so or not. It is false teaching. It sounds good. It looks good. It may even seem like love. However, when it does not fall in line with God's Word, it is not love, it is destruction; it is not light, it is darkness.

There is yet another "Jesus" being proclaimed aside from Lucifer's mythological guise, and I would call him the "New Age Jesus." This "Jesus" does not preach a God-centered gospel but a man-centered one. You can find this "Jesus" in megachurches across the country, in

The Chosen TV series, and in Contemporary Christian Music, though these are not the only places we hear about him. This "Jesus" does not condemn sin. Rather, this "Jesus" accepts you along with your sin and declares peace for everyone regardless of sincere repentance. This is not the Jesus of the Bible. This "Jesus" does not care if you are Christian, Hindu, Buddhist, Mormon, Catholic, Muslim, Jew, or whatever. In this train of thought, all paths lead to the same God. This simply is not true. It is not biblical. Wide is the gate that leads to destruction. Narrow is the gate that leads to life. This "Jesus" is nothing more than Lucifer in Jesus clothing. We are all God's children, says this "Jesus." Correction. We are all God's creation, but we are not all God's children. We must be born again to be a part of His family. This means we cannot merely be born of water in the flesh; we must also be born of the Spirit. This only comes through reconciliation by faith in the blood of Jesus Christ and true repentance. Whoever rejects this truth will be rejected.

Some may say, well, I don't want to serve a God who would send someone to hell over "little" sins and a few bad choices. To that, I would say, I don't want to serve a God who would allow an eternity in heaven with a little bit of sin, a little bit of darkness. I wouldn't want that any more than I would want to eat a brownie with a little bit of excrement in it. A little leaven leavens the whole lump. A "little" sin corrupts the entire system. He would not be a good or a just God if He overlooked a "little" sin. Sin must be paid for, and the wages of sin is death. If we reject the atoning death and resurrection of Jesus Christ, if we refuse to accept this truth and refuse to allow Him to be Lord (master and ruler) of our lives, we must pay the price ourselves. I recently heard a pastor retell a story which speaks to this point, and the bottom line was this: We have all been born into sin, so we all have sin within us. The price for sin is death. The payment for that sin is either *on* Jesus Christ or it is *on* you.

This "Jesus" (Lucifer) is attempting to unite all religions in the name of "unity" and "love." It is true that God is love. However, you cannot have true love apart from justice. He would not be a loving God if He were not also a just God. He cannot and will not let sin go unpunished. Thankfully, He has paid our price and has freely offered us the gift of salvation; it is up to us to accept His gift through faith and repentance.

These all-inclusive universalist heresies are sending souls to hell forever, and the scriptures are being completely distorted in the name of "unity" and "love." We need to stay grounded in the Word of God and pray for discernment because it is getting crazy out there. The deceptive garbage being circulated among so-called Christians is both subtle and deadly. I find it both telling and interesting that the verses which talk about loving one another because God is love, in I John 4, are directly preceded with the verses which talk about testing the spirits because many false prophets have gone out into the world.

In addition to staying close to the LORD, we ought to be sharing our hope with whomever will listen. We ought to pray diligently for God to lead us to those whom He is seeking. We ought to pray for boldness and clarity of speech to proclaim the hope we have found in Christ alone. We need to pray for God to give us compassion to reach out to those who are lost. We need to pray for God to help us live as salt and light.

We also need to be actively discipling those whom God places in our lives. Jesus said, "Go, and make disciples of all nations." We should be encouraging one another to grow in the grace and knowledge of our Lord Jesus Christ through reading God's Word, obeying God's Word, and sincere and constant prayer from the heart. It is not about the number of "converts." If I "lead someone to Jesus" but do not disciple them in the ways of maturity, what have I accomplished? What happens when the fire fizzles and the euphoria dies? It is not about quantity but quality.

If you are thinking to yourself, I have difficulty talking to people or I have social anxiety, you are not alone, but do not let that stop you. I have seen Christ do through me things I never could have done on my own. He is able to do immeasurably more than we can ask or imagine, and He will enable you to do all that He calls you to do. I am fully introvert, so the second I find myself in a conversation with someone, I am looking for the quickest way out of it. Small talk and interacting with others is completely draining to me, but it is necessary, and the LORD supplies the strength.

There are many ways to scatter seeds and proclaim the gospel of Christ. I have mentioned to you previously something I have done with handwritten cards, and I would like to post a challenge to you! The challenge is this: Make five to ten of your own cards and hand them out as the LORD leads you to do so. When you run out, make some more. On the front of a 5 x 7 index card, write the gospel out in plain terms. On the back, write a short version of your testimony.

Pray as you are writing them that God would begin now to work in the hearts of the people who will receive them. He knows who is going to get those cards, and you can begin to pray for those people even before you know who they are. Keep them in your purse or car or whatever, and when you leave the house, pray that God would open a door to give out a card. Pray that He would soften their hearts to receive His truth. Pray for the Holy Spirit to lead the conversation.

When you give it out, try to incorporate an act of kindness along with it. Maybe it is monetary; maybe it is not. It is whatever God lays on your heart. Maybe you have an acquaintance or a neighbor for whom you could cook a meal or bake cookies. Make sure to give them a card too! It is a nonintrusive way to share your faith and possibly open a door for future meaningful conversations. Once you hand it to them, ask them, "Is there anything for which I can pray for you?" Then, as you are walking or driving away, pray for them. Pray for their reconciliation to God and that God would speak to their heart in that special way only He can. It has been such a blessing to do this over the past couple of years. On several occasions, I have seen some of the recipients again, and I know that it has been effective. Do not do this in your own strength, however. Pray. A lot. Talking to God throughout the process is essential.

A handwritten card means something to lots of people, and every one of you has your own beautiful story of transformation. To God be the glory! So make some cards and share your hope with those whom God places in your path! They desperately need what you have, so make the best use of your time because the days are evil.

- Let us test and examine our ways and return to the LORD! (Lamentations 3:40).
- For it will come upon all who dwell on the face of the earth, but stay awake at all times, praying that you may have strength to escape all

these things that are going to take place and to stand before the Son of Man (Luke 21:34-36).

- For still the vision awaits its appointed time. It hastens to the end – it will not lie. If it seems slow, wait for it. It will surely come – it will not delay (Habakkuk 2:3).
- Therefore, my beloved brothers and sisters, be steadfast, immovable, always abounding in the work of the LORD, knowing that in the LORD, your labor is not in vain (I Corinthians 15:58).
- Seek the LORD, all you humble of the land, who do His just commands; seek righteousness; seek humility; perhaps you may be hidden on the day of the anger of the LORD (Zephaniah 2:3).

The end of the matter; all has been heard. Fear God and keep His commandments, for this is the whole duty of man. For God will bring every deed into judgment, with every secret thing, whether good or evil (Ecclesiastes 12:13-14).

Just a Note:

As you learned from my testimony,
I do not have any sort of online platform,
so this is purely and simply a word-of-mouth project.
If you know someone who might benefit from reading this
book, please join me in getting the word out!
Thank You

WORKS CITED

Josephus – M'Clatchie, "Notes and Queries on China and Japan" (edited by Dennys), Vol 4, Nos 7,8, P. 100.

"Turn Your Eyes Upon Jesus" by Lemmel, Helen (author). 1922. Public Domain, hymn.

"God Will Make a Way" by Don Moen. © 1990 Integrity's Hosanna! Music (ASCAP) (adm at IntegratedRights.com). All rights reserved. Used by permission.

Smith, Bertha. *How the Spirit Filled My Life*. Broadman Press, January 1, 1973.

Harari, Yuval Noah. Interview by Noema with Worldpost at Berggruen Institute, Los Angeles. March 24, 2017. *www.noemamag.com*. "Human History Will End When Men Become Gods."

Harari, Yuval Noah. Interview by GE Breakthrough reports. November 15, 2015. *www.ge.com*. "Are Humans Becoming More God-Like?"

Spurgeon, Charles H. Sermon quote